SOMEONE IS MISSING

SOMEONE IS MISSING

A MEMOIR

Sonia Melchett

WEIDENFELD AND NICOLSON · LONDON

920. MEL

First published in Great Britain in 1987 by
George Weidenfeld & Nicolson Limited
91 Clapham High Street, London SW4 7TA

ISBN 0 297 79129 X

Photoset, printed and bound in Great Britain by
Redwood Burn Limited, Trowbridge, Wiltshire

For Andrew

Author's Note

The following account is based on my own experiences, although I have disguised some of the characters to protect their privacy.

PART ONE

Go, go, go, said the bird; human kind
Cannot bear very much reality.

T. S. Eliot, *Four Quartets*, 'Burnt Norton'

CHAPTER 1

The bell rang all round the school. Each girl stopped whatever she was doing to listen. The bell only rang to summon someone to the Head Mistress's study. The daughter didn't hear it; she was clearing out her guinea-pig hutch. At this school they were allowed to keep pets as long as they took total responsibility for their welfare, and the daughter's guinea-pigs were particularly well cared for. At the beginning of term she had persuaded her father to let her bring two sacks of hay from their farm in Norfolk and her mother had driven her to school with the hay in the boot of the car together with all the paraphernalia required by a girl boarding at a progressive upper-class school in 1973.

Someone called, 'It's for you, the Snail's calling you.'

The daughter felt a twinge of fear. She wasn't the most law-abiding schoolgirl – in fact one could say she was a non-conformist. A mistress discussing her in the Common Room once said: 'I enjoy teaching her. She has an original mind. She questions everything.' Another observed: 'That child has been spoilt. It's a pity – she has a good brain, but it is totally undisciplined.'

The daughter finished what she was doing: she put fresh hay into the hutch, she refilled the saucer with water, she kissed the guinea-pigs and closed the latch. As she walked slowly towards the Snail's study, she examined her conscience. It couldn't be the radio she had smuggled into school.

That had already been confiscated. It couldn't be smoking pot or cigarettes: she had tried both, but hadn't really enjoyed either. Of course it was the boys. Only yesterday she had persuaded her greatest friend, a rather timid girl, that it would be a good idea to skip the early morning run, a compulsory mile round the grounds before breakfast. The two of them could go instead through the gap in the hedge to see if they could catch a glimpse of any of the village boys. It had been an unsuccessful enterprise. They only caught a furtive glimpse of Tom, the newspaper boy, as he passed them on his bike without noticing their existence. As far as she knew the adventure had been unobserved, but now, as she knocked on the large oak door leading from the library, she was already preparing her answers. 'I'm really sorry, Miss Banks. I know it was very wrong of me. . . .' The Snail was standing with her back to her looking out of the window towards the large copper beech at the far end of the rose garden. When she turned round the daughter felt herself trembling. The Snail looked really severe. What could it be?

'Come and sit down, my dear,' she said, and gently led her to a chintz-covered sofa at one side of the fireplace. 'I'm afraid I have some very sad news for you.'

The daughter felt relieved. Sad news. Then she wasn't to be punished.

'Your father died this morning in Majorca.'

Your father died this morning in Majorca. The words resounded in her head without her accepting they were so.

'Have this – it will help.' She sipped something very nasty from a cut-glass tumbler. 'I'm sorry you should have to hear this from me, but your mother was unable to get in touch. She was afraid you might see something on television.'

The daughter put the glass with its bitter drink on the polished table and stood facing the Head Mistress.

'Yes, I understand, thank you. Where's Mummy?'

'She is flying back tonight and the chauffeur is on his way

4

down to collect you and take you to meet her. Your brother and sister will be with him.' The Snail suddenly leant towards her and gave her a peck on the cheek. 'You must be very brave.'

You must be very brave. 'Yes, thank you. I'll try.' She turned and almost ran from the room. The Junior loo was on the same floor. She went in and locked the door. 'Why aren't I crying? Daddy is dead. Daddy is dead. But it's not true. It can't be.' She thought of the last days of the holidays. He and she had ridden all round the farm. He always talked to her between gallops. That field of barley had greenfly this year – it would have to be sprayed – there was a dead tree in one of the woods. He carried a notebook in his pocket and dropped the reins of his large grey horse and took notes for the farm foreman. Suddenly the tears gushed down her face. It couldn't be true. Then she felt a sharp pain in the pit of her stomach. Mummy will die too, she couldn't exist without Daddy. She had never really thought of them separately, always together as a pair, like her guinea-pigs. She went to find Sarah. But when she opened the loo door Sarah was already there. She knew.

'What is going to happen? Are you going away?' She looked so forlorn, the daughter had to comfort her.

'Yes, but probably only for a short time. Will you look after the guinea-pigs until I come back?'

'Of course.' Their eyes met. Sarah's eyes were full of tears. The daughter stopped crying.

'Mummy's flying home. We are all going to meet her at an airfield.'

The car arrived with her brother and elder sister driven by Ron. Dear Ron, usually so full of jokes and cockney rhyming slang. She noticed his eyes were red as he kissed her and then put her luggage in the boot and helped her in. As they sped through the night to the airfield, the brother was on the car telephone trying to reach his grandmother to give the news to her before she heard it on the radio or saw it on television. The father had been a public figure.

'But what happened?' she asked her sister.

'We don't know. It was a heart attack, I think, but the line from Majorca was so bad...' and the sister started sobbing. The brother had one hand covering his ear while he tried to talk on the telephone: 'Please, I can't hear. Yes, we think it was a heart attack, but we don't really know. The press have been on to you already have they? I'm sorry. I did try to call you before we set off for the school, but the line was engaged. I'm sorry.' The brother leaned back. He looked pale and exhausted. He closed his eyes.

CHAPTER 2

As the twin-engined executive jet flew through the night sky
the mother sat in the front seat on the right. Opposite her was
the husband's secretary, notebook on her lap, taking shorthand from the man who was now acting as Chairman of the
Corporation. His wife was sitting next to him. The mother
was looking at the stars, more beautiful than she had ever
remembered seeing them before. The pain accumulated.
Twenty-four hours ago in sunlight the husband had been
where the secretary was now sitting. She had looked across at
him at one moment when he was laughing with the Deputy-
Chairman. They had come through a difficult period with the
business and had recently had a successful breakthrough. She
had thought how well he looked. He was still brown from the
previous weekend they had spent in Venice.

Venice – it seemed years ago already. They had gone out to
the Cipriani for a business conference, but had stayed on two
more days to be alone ; they had spent their honeymoon there
twenty-four years before. One night they had dined out on
Torcello and sped back across the lagoon through a thick
layer of mist lying over the water. He had his arm round her
for warmth. She had looked across the haze and had thought,
'It will always be like this. We will always be together now.'
She felt a joy of rare calm and the conviction that all was well.

That night their lovemaking was passionate, and she had
slept in his arms in one of the twin beds of their room. In the

7

morning, before he woke, she crept into the other bed and slept again. They had gone to the Lido later that day to swim and lie in the sun. They had looked at the pictures in the Doge's Palace. It was strange, the Hieronymous Bosch, with the little people on the end of the world. The husband had wanted to leave. He felt a little tired. 'It's the heat,' she said. After dinner they had sat at a small round table in St Mark's Square and had bought two yo-yos from a small boy. They had walked back to their hotel arm in arm playing with the yo-yos with their free hands. She had been drowsy and happy. It would always be so.

But now she was in an aeroplane, with the noise of engines. Tears were running down her face uncontrollably and she made no attempt to wipe them away. The other woman said to the acting Chairman: 'Must you go into all that now? You're upsetting her.' But the mother hardly heard. Her mind was going back over the last twenty-four hours as it had already done time after time and would do again and again. That same morning they had all arrived at Palma airport for a working weekend. The Deputy-Chairman and his wife had gone into the town to do some shopping and would join them later. Outside the airport they were met by a car driven by the gardener of their villa. The husband had sat in the front of the car and she directly behind him next to the secretary. His left arm was resting across the back of the seat as he turned round to talk to them. The sleeve of his blue shirt was rolled up and the blond hairs showed on his brown arm. He was happy and excited to be revisiting their villa in Formentor, which they had planned and built together ten years before, cutting down the size of the bedrooms as they worked out the price in pesetas per square metre. This was during the days before he was earning a large salary. They had saved a little money and decided to spend it on building a summer house. But they had always been reckless about money. When they had married they had used nearly all their capital from his grandmother to

8

buy the lease of a flat in an unfashionable part of London. His parents had been rich, but there had been quarrels. They had thought her too young; but he had been determined to marry her and had soon found a job.

As he turned in the car to tell her something, their eyes met. She knew they would make love that day. She spoke to the secretary, knowing she was excluded from their happiness.

They drove for an hour. The last stretch of the road was precipitous, winding round the side of a mountain. At the top, cars were parked overlooking the view. She had never liked that view, too spectacular, like a glossy postcard. The superlatives which bubbled from people when they first saw it were predictable and grated on her nerves. They passed the hotel with its formal flowerbeds and uniformed porters taking in expensive luggage, and drove up a steep road rough with craters and boulders. There was an unending battle between the hotel and the owners of the half-dozen villas about the state of the road. The owners preferred to keep it virtually unusable to deter the encroaching tourists: the hotel wanted it repaired, but wasn't prepared to pay.

As they pulled up at the small iron gate of their house, it was immediately opened by a stout smiling woman, the gardener's wife. Greetings and news of children were exchanged in Spanish. She followed the husband under the stone archway through to the large cool terrace, where lunch was laid out on the wooden table. The sunlight made beautiful patterns through the slatted green cover.

'Do you want to eat straight away or shall we swim first?' she asked. But the husband was already halfway down the steep uneven steps which led through the oleander, bougainvillaea and plumbago. The secretary said she would wait for them. The wife grabbed a bikini and swimming trunks from their luggage and followed him down. She sat on the flat jetty dangling her feet in the water.

'Icy,' she said, but he had already dived in and started

swimming towards the tiny island about a quarter of a mile away. At the half-way point a rock stuck out of the water. He had climbed on to it and called out to her as she was about to pass by.

'Don't be in such a rush – stop and give me a kiss.' She sat on the rock for a moment and felt a deep contentment. This villa, their creation, had been the scene of many a family drama. It had been witness to the different phases of their marriage, the disappointments in his career, their occasional infidelities and following jealousies. But today the calm clear blue water reflected her mood of transparent happiness. She swam to the island and, when she got back to the jetty below the house, he had put on his swimming trunks and was lying face downwards to soak in the sun. She lay down beside him for a moment and realized by a gentle snore that he had gone to sleep.

'Darling, wake up. Let's have lunch.'

Silence. She prodded him. No movement. A wild panic possessed her as she looked at his immobile body. She used all her strength to turn him over. She put her ear to his heart. He seemed to be breathing. As she tore up the steps calling the secretary to telephone for a doctor she thought, It's not true – it can't be happening. Her bikini top was dangling round her neck – how ridiculous she must look – how could she think of something like that now?

She grabbed the pills which his heart specialist had prescribed, found some water and rushed back down the steps followed by the gardener and his wife. As she tried to get him to swallow the pills, she felt helpless and futile. What should she be doing? She tried the kiss of life, which she'd never been taught. She tried massaging his heart. She thought he was just breathing. All the time the sun was beating mercilessly on to the rock. The half hour it took the doctor to arrive from the village was the worst in her life, but after an eternity he was there.

'I think he's still alive,' the doctor said. 'Look for a large flat stone while I massage his heart.'

'A large flat stone? What on earth for?'

'To put under his head.'

The only stones she could see were small and round. When she found a flat one, she brought it to the doctor. The gardener's wife was weeping.

'I'm afraid he's dead,' said the doctor.

'No,' she said. 'We must get him to hospital. There must be something to be done.'

He took her arm leading her up the steps. 'There's nothing anyone can do. It was a massive coronary. I will make all the arrangements.'

She stood on the terrace and, as if in a trance, watched as they carried the inert body in a canvas chair up the steep steps to lay it in her bedroom. Suddenly a woman from a neighbouring villa was holding her hand and saying words to comfort her. They hardly knew each other. They had certainly never been friends. Why was this stranger here now? All she wanted was to be left alone.

CHAPTER 3

The jet landed at a small private airfield, to avoid the press and publicity. The three children waited for the mother to appear. They ran towards her. She flung open the cloak she was wearing and tried to envelop them within it, and they stood clinging to each other without speaking for several minutes. Then she noticed Ron, the driver, standing forlornly by the car.

'Let's go home,' she said.

Driving through the night back to London, she told them in broken sentences of their father's death. The son, sitting next to Ron in the front, turned round to ask something. She thought : but it couldn't have been only this morning that the same older eyes had turned to look into hers. Half of her was coping with their questions and comforting her daughters, but the other half was a jagged aching void, still not accepting, refusing to accept – it must be a nightmare from which she must wake. But the nightmare went on. There would be no waking.

Back at the house their 'daily' opened the door. For once she was speechless – the tiny, gallant woman who had worked for her, shared her disappointments and triumphs, who revelled in minor disasters and turned them into jokes, was subdued and almost distant.

'Here's a letter from the Palace,' she said.

The mother opened it in disbelief and read the brief words of condolence, thinking – how efficient to be so quick; and then – how thoughtful.

'I'll get you a nice cup of tea, dear,' the 'daily' said. But there were things to be talked over and arrangements to be made. The husband's body must be brought back to England. She made the son promise to fly out to Majorca to bring the coffin back. He thought it was unnecessary and that she was being unreasonable. She became hysterical.

'You can't let him come back all alone. If you won't do it, I'll go myself.'

But he knew, and she knew, that she wouldn't be able to face it. 'Of course I'll go,' he said. He would have to shoulder many responsibilities in the coming months and years – this, his first duty.

The next few days and nights were blurred. She took pills to steal a few hours of oblivion. She refused food, but people said, 'You must make yourself eat. You must think of the children.' Cups of tea and hot milk were given after road accidents – it eased the ends of the nerves. In her daze, she felt mutilated, as if only a part of her were left. A philosopher had once said the world only existed in the eyes of God and that matter had no real existence. She had existed because one man had believed in her. Now she had no existence. Friends wrote and telephoned and sent her books . . . books by doctors and philosophers . . . come to terms with your grief . . . give in to it . . . Americans had invented the best expression, 'Let it all hang out.' But this she found impossible – perhaps it was her upbringing. Brought up in India, the child of an Army doctor, she had become used to seeing the greatest of human miseries. Her father had taken her round the hospital wards when she was six years old. When she or her younger sister had suffered from the minor complaints of childhood, they knew what to expect from their father. Sweat out a fever, feed a cold, eat an apple a day, keep the bowels open. He only gave pills to patients who believed that the brightly coloured capsules were a magic cure – and so they cured. But their *ayah* listened to their moans and groans with sympathy and gave them betel-nutty kisses.

She had one close woman friend, a woman of great beauty and intelligence, but who suffered from an instinct for self-destruction – a divorcee who had survived a nervous break-down. They had many shared experiences, children and holidays, even a lover. She would understand. She had known them both well, she had even had a brief affair with the husband. People couldn't understand how their friend-ship had survived this act of betrayal.

'I feel I'm acting a part,' she told the friend. 'I was never made for tragedy, I don't know how to behave. I even resent him for being dead. I can't forgive him for deserting me, for turning me into an object of pity ... a widow.' How she already hated that word, which always conjured up aged sad silver-haired old ladies. 'I'm playing a role for which I'm totally unsuited, totally unrehearsed.' Her previous roles had all been positive, full of optimism, excitement and challenge. Disappointments and minor tragedies, yes, but always to be shared.

'I understand,' the friend said, 'but you're stronger than you realize. Somehow you will slowly learn to weave him into the fabric of your life. But now, after such a short time, I know how you must feel. Unhappiness is like being in love, it isolates. Grief never contaminates, though you may feel like a leper.'

The friend helped her with all the practical details sur-rounding a death. The funeral was in a private family mauso-leum in St John's Wood. He had been a Fleet Air Arm pilot at the end of the war, so the coffin was covered with a Royal Navy flag; it was surrounded by a handful of relations, most of whom had not been particularly fond of either of them.

The mother-in-law had never forgiven the younger son for living after her elder and favourite son had been killed during the last weeks of the war: she had also nursed her husband through a serious illness before he, too, had died.

After the short service, they left the dark damp mausoleum and stepped outside into brilliant sunshine. Through her tears, the wife saw the daffodils in profusion all around them. With the heightened sensibility and awareness that grieving brings, she felt the world had never shone with such brilliance or hurt more intensely.

An ex-colleague of the husband suggested she borrow his house in the South of France for a fortnight, and the friend said she would go with her. This practical gesture of help was a temporary lifeline, but before they left there were a million things to do. The first thing was to give away his clothes. She couldn't bear to see them hanging neatly in their bedroom. She gave everything away, his watch, his cuff-links, his hair-brushes. She was amazed at how little there was. He had always been ruthless at keeping his personal possessions to a minimum.

'Don't you want to keep anything?' people asked in shocked voices. On the table by their bed, she kept the book with the red leather marker showing the page he had been reading before they left London. She kept all his photographs and letters, and the albums she had spent many a contented hour pasting in happy holiday reminders of children and friends and press-cuttings – a potted history of their life together. These she kept, although she wouldn't have the courage to look at them again for a long time. The last album had only just been begun and the final pages would remain blank for ever.

There were the will and bequests to deal with. Everything was in immaculate order. He had left her well provided for, with a short impersonal letter to her in his own hand warning her to keep away from expensive solicitors. Once, in Norfolk walking round their farm, he had tried to explain about the will. She had refused to discuss it, thinking it morbid. Now she was relieved that everything was so clear and straightforward.

She had to go to the Norfolk farm, to see the people who had worked for him and give them their gifts. Give, give – it was easy – what need had she of possessions when her whole reason for living had suddenly gone? All the things they had bought for each other as gifts to demonstrate their love now seemed superfluous. We possess through our posessions. In divorce when there is bitterness, possessions are used as weapons to hurt and dispossess. The giving was easy. More difficult was having to stay in the house they had converted together fifteen years before. A farmhouse surrounded by acres of crops – barley, sugar-beet, lucerne. A typical Norfolk coastal farm. But they had made the house in their own style, a large upstairs living-room with a raised fireplace set into the original rough white brick wall. A bay window looking on to a garden full of untidy shrub roses, peonies and lilac and apple trees; and, through the gap in the wall, the fields beyond and then the sea.

That evening, as it was beginning to grow dark, she walked through the garden, through the gap in the wall and down towards the sea. If only she could just go on walking for ever. She lay on the damp grass and remembered another evening. She had been staying at the farm with the children during their school holidays. He had arrived late one Friday from London looking exhausted after a week of unsuccessful business negotiations. She had led him into the garden to show him something of which she was proud. It was a climbing 'Rosa Philippe', a tiny white rose she had planted to grow up an old apple tree. She had got the idea after a visit to the white and blue gardens of Sissinghurst.

'Look, it's worked,' she said. The tiny clusters of roses were showering over the top of the old tree like an enormous umbrella.

'And you said you'd never be a gardener,' he replied. 'It's beautiful.' But she knew he was really looking at the crops beyond the garden, through the gap in the wall to the edge of the barley field. Suddenly the clouds had cleared and a full moon bathed the farm in light and the dew glistened on the damp grass. They didn't speak, but the magic was all around them. For years they had worked to build their lives . . . children, professions, friendships, houses. She had supported him in all his radical efforts to fight injustice wherever he met it. That night, perhaps because of the magic, they both felt a sense of fulfilment and awe.

She realized she had been lying on the damp grass for ages. Her dress was soaked through. She walked slowly back to the house and to the small guest bedroom in the back where she had chosen to sleep. She passed the two portraits, painted by a friend who was now a well-known artist. They had been very young and their eyes looking out from the canvases were cold and impersonal. 'Who are these people? Nothing to do with me.' That night she lay awake, drained, unloved, unloving. Then a fierce feeling of hatred invaded her, hatred for this house, for that garden, for a God whose cruelty could be so random, but most of all, hatred for herself. The bitterness mounted. Suddenly she saw clearly what she must do. Of course, it was so logical. She went to the kitchen and took the sharpest knife she could find. She carefully took the portraits down from the wall. She slashed first her face, the cold eyes, the young smiling mouth. Cut – cut – the canvas was difficult to destroy, but she was feeling strong. She cut until her arm ached. Then she turned to the husband. Yes, he must be destroyed, too: one could not live without the other. But something stopped her cutting into his face. Instead she slashed all around it, until the portrait was an unrecognizable object.

Back in bed she felt almost peaceful. They will say, 'She went mad. She did it in a moment of madness.' But it wasn't madness. It was just something she had to do.

CHAPTER 4

In London, the outside world continued as before. Stepping off the train at Liverpool Street Station, she could recognize that life was going on as usual, but she could no longer see it in the same way. Everything seemed to have changed and taken on a new significance. Travelling through the City, she was transfixed by the beauty of St Paul's, Wren's great dome in its crowded isolation. Driving along the Embankment, the river glittered under the opalescence of the clouds. The world had never been so defined and so distant. The laughter of children came from far streets. She seemed to have stepped outside life and didn't know how to step back. Her whole being was on the wrong side of the looking-glass.

The letters continued to pour in: most were spontaneous, generous and emotional. They said he had been much too young to die. All his virtues were listed, his courage, his vision, his sense of humour. The letters all helped, but the ones which helped her most also spoke of her, of her virtues, of what she had meant to him and of the future, a future in which she had somehow to make herself believe. The obituaries in the national newspapers were fulsome in their praise. She put them all away in the top of a cupboard.

The younger daughter had returned to boarding school. It had seemed harsh, but at the time the best solution. Later she had decided to try and get her into a day school in London, so that at least they could be of some comfort to each other.

There was to be a Memorial Service in Westminster Abbey, and a lot of planning was involved. The mother and the two older children went to the Chapter Office to meet the Dean and the Chaplain to discuss the protocol and the details of the service. They sat round a long refectory table with pads of paper and pencils neatly arranged as if for a board meeting. The clergy were solicitous and thorough. 'This must be commonplace to them,' she thought, 'just a routine.' One half of her was listening and appreciating their attention to detail. There were to be Government representatives, many important business associates from overseas. Seats had to be allocated. 'I won't be able to face it,' she thought. 'Why should I? I'll just go away.' But she knew it would be an act of desertion. She owed it to him to observe the conventions of her faith, such as it was, which required her to fulfil this final obligation.

'And the music and hymns? Have you any preferences or will you leave it to us?' She realized they were asking her questions.

'We'll let you know,' the son said, 'when we've given it some thought.'

Going home in the taxi the three of them suggested hymns to each other and sang snatches of their favourites. The elder daughter had a good voice and was singing the opening bars of Blake's beautiful hymn 'And did those feet in ancient time'. The taxi driver turned his head. 'That's one of my favourites,' he said. 'Been to a wedding, have you?'

Before the Service took place, she and the friend went to the house she had been lent in the South of France for a week. They hired a car and drove from Nice airport along the coast to the little villa on the outskirts of Villefranche. She took all the letters of condolence with her and every morning was spent replying to them. Sometimes she was overcome by the raw shock as if she had undergone a mammoth amputation.

At such moments she thought of suicide. It would be so easy. The pull of oblivion was almost overwhelming. But she knew that to give up the game would be total cowardice, inflicting a further terrible wound on the children and her own elderly mother.

It did not seem possible that the days could move on relentlessly as they did. In the afternoons she would walk down to the little public beach below the villa. One hot day, with the sun blazing down on the pebbles, she took her first faltering steps into the sea. She had always loved swimming, but now her movements were those of a puppet. She wanted to swim far out, but there were white buoys bobbing on the water protecting the swimmers from the speedboats. Back on the beach, she lay on her towel, hardly aware of the pebbles pressing into her skin. A French couple were helping their children build a sandcastle by the water's edge. It was a beach scene she had taken part in and witnessed a thousand times, but now she saw it in an exaggerated clarity as if for the first time. The serious expression on the boy's face as he patted the sand into the bucket and tipped it carefully on to the castle. The little girl emptying buckets of water into the moat. The father was enjoying himself, but the young mother was bored and went back to her magazine. The scene was one of such ordinary contentment that she wanted to scream out, 'Don't take it all so for granted. Don't you realize you're a complete family? It may never be like this again.'

Sometimes in the evenings they drove to the hill towns above the coast to dine in bistros under pergolas covered with wistaria. Everywhere she looked, she was aware of couples: flirting young couples more engrossed in each other than their food; elderly married couples, comfortably silent, eating and drinking with total concentration; gays in earnest conversation.

'They probably think we're lesbians,' the friend said.

They talked of the future. She would have to work, but had

so few qualifications. She had been an assistant to a BBC producer briefly before her marriage. She remembered once writing in her diary, 'Since everything man needs has to be discovered by his own mind and produced by his own efforts, the two essentials of the method of survival proper to a rational being are thinking and productive work.' Yes, she would have to try and find work, but for now she could only just limp through each day with its anxieties bordering on panic. The nights were the worst. The doctor had prescribed pills, but, after two or three hours of drugged sleep, the nightmares started. She never dreamt of him, yet the themes were recurrent ones of physical struggle against impossible odds, and sometimes she would wake sweating with fear. The day always began as if there were a thick wall of fog which she had somehow to break through.

Drink numbed the pain, when it became unbearable. This she knew was considered cowardly and was merely postponing the day when life would have to be faced in all its rawness. But why was it so terrible? You put sticking plaster over a wound to stop the bleeding, a temporary dressing until the skin healed itself. Was it so wrong to use any available means to assuage the internal bleeding of a creature in torment?

Back in London there were the final arrangements to be made for the Service. A bus to bring people from the farm. Seats to be allocated to VIPs in the correct pecking order. The younger daughter to be brought back from school. When the day arrived, she realized that she had nothing in black suitable to wear. She found a dark brown suit, once a perfect fit, which now hung loosely on her thin body, and she wound a scarf round her head. What did it matter? What did anything matter except getting through the ceremony with some dignity? The conventions of life seemed without any significance.

As she and the children walked into the Abbey the organist was playing music from Bach and Handel, and they took their seats in the front row of the West Transept. She was aware of a host of familiar and unfamiliar faces, their blank expressions controlling any emotions in the true British tradition. As the choir broke into 'I will lift up mine eyes unto the hills: from whence cometh my help', the elder daughter started to cry.

'Not here, you mustn't,' whispered her sister. 'Later, you can.'

The Dean ended the Service with:

No man is an island, entire of itself;
Every man is a piece of the continent, a part of the main.
The death of one diminishes all.
For all are bound together in the bundle of life.

She was trying to read the last page of the Order of Service: 'All shall remain kneeling and the choir shall sing "God be in my head, and in my understanding..." Then shall the Bells of the Abbey Church be rung, half-muffled.... The congregation are requested to remain in their seats until directed by the stewards to move.'

The son took her arm and gently steered her through the Abbey. She was clear-eyed and held her head high. Outside, people surrounded her, took her hands, kissed her. Many had tears in their eyes. He had been much loved.

CHAPTER 5

As the weeks passed she and the younger daughter tried to settle into their new roles. The daughter, normally so extrovert and ebullient, had become withdrawn and difficult. She would take the bus to her new school every morning and the mother would collect her by car in the afternoon. Waiting for the school gates to open were other parents, standing around chatting happily to each other. Some of them she knew slightly, but she remained in the car pretending to read a book. She couldn't bear the flicker of embarrassed awareness in the eyes of others, that moment when they couldn't decide whether or not to mention the death. Why is it that the bereaved are treated as outcasts? As the girls started to push through the gates in laughing groups in their grey coats, a jumble of tennis rackets, violin cases and satchels, her eyes searched for the daughter, hoping that she, too, would be among the main throng. But she never was. She came out later, alone, white-faced, and walked straight towards the car.

'It's no good, I can't stand it,' she said. 'The work's too difficult and none of the girls in my form like me.'

'Nonsense, of course they like you. It's your imagination, darling.' Her false, cheerful voice prattled on with advice and optimistic predictions, but the daughter looked unbelieving and hid in a silent privacy of resistance.

Later she would try and help with the homework, but

found some of the new methods of teaching difficult to grasp.

At half-term they were invited to stay with friends in Scotland for a few days. The families had never been particularly close and she was surprised by the invitation, but in her present mood of fatality she drifted with gratitude into any challenge and escape from the silent house. In the past she had sometimes longed for periods of solitude within a frenetic life, but now that she was alone, she felt differently.

They flew to Inverness and were met by a cheerful man with a rugged face, wearing a kilt in the tartan of his laird's clan. They drove along narrow winding roads past the castle which one day would be inherited by their host, and over a small bridge to the dower house, a grey stone shooting lodge on an island surrounded by water the colour of peat.

In spite of the parents' solicitous tact to the mother and the warm welcome their children gave to the daughter, the visit did not go well.

There were two other guests, philosophers from Cambridge. At the first dinner in the shabby grand dining-room, with the children at the far end of the table, the talk veered from political and university gossip to a dissertation from one of the dons on his interpretation of 'structuralism'. The more she tried to contribute to the conversation, the more banal her words seemed. Without his presence to support her and his love to give her self-confidence, she felt inadequate. After dinner they put Verdi's *Requiem* on the record player. It was one of her favourite pieces and she sank back into the faded chintz chair to enjoy the first movement with its melodies so full of restraint and piety and yet strangely sensual. But towards the end of the Kyrie when the choral music reaches its joyful climax, she suddenly felt the tears course down her face. She rushed from the room along endless corridors to the guest bedroom. Later the host appeared with words of sympathy and a cup of hot milk.

'Have this. I've put a dram into it – do you nothing but

good. Sorry to have been so long, but it's some time since I've rummaged around the kitchens.' He stood by her bed, tall and splendid in his velvet jacket and tartan trousers. 'Did you know that one of the dons is doing a thesis on the effect of certain pieces of classical music on the emotions – how some particular themes can trigger off certain emotions? Of course, we didn't foresee the effect when we played that piece of music, but you've certainly proved his point. He's full of remorse.'

She found she was smiling. 'As automatic as a Pavlov dog,' she said. 'Tell him not to worry. I'm glad I've been of some use.'

In the aeroplane going home, they swapped stories about the visit. She hoped, anyway, the daughter had enjoyed it.

'I was sick,' she said.

'Sick?' the mother repeated.

'Yes, on the way to the dining-room on the first night. Sick with fright.' She looked accusingly at the mother. 'You know, the elder girl is just like a grown-up. She keeps a bottle of vodka in her room. We all had to drink it. Anyway, as long as you had a good time.' And she remained buried in Sylvia Plath for the rest of the flight. Neither of them had been ready for normal family life.

On inheriting the father's title, the son had taken his seat in the Lords. He had been reluctant at first as he was a Labour Party supporter and didn't approve of hereditary titles, but he had been persuaded that the best way to fight for his convictions was from within the Establishment. He made no concessions in his lifestyle. He would ride to the Lords on his motorbike, leaving it in the Peers' car park, putting on a tie as he passed the top-hatted attendants. He soon became completely at ease with the formalities and traditions of the Upper House, and began to make a reputation as a formidable speaker and a committed Socialist. He, her first-born, had always been sensitive to the mother's needs, the bond between them as strong as the umbilical cord. Now, since the father's death, she knew he had to make the final break.

The elder daughter was living outside Norwich in a cottage with her boyfriend and taking a degree in Development Studies at the University of East Anglia. She became more and more involved with the problems of the oppressed peoples of the Third World, ground down and exploited by the great multinational companies of the West. A new generation was emerging from the universities, citizens of the world without national pride or patriotism, passionately anti-nuclear, critical of their parents, taking for granted as their heritage the benefits of the Welfare State, for which those parents had fought. The drug culture flourished, creating further rifts between the generations. Parents guiltily sipped their gin-and-tonics, while being lectured on the virtues of pot and the horrors of alcohol. The mother thought she was fortunate that none of her children had drifted into the hard drug scene. She had seen the children of some of her friends destroying themselves on the slippery slopes of addiction.

In trying to pick up the pieces of her life she started accepting invitations to drinks, to dinners, even to a dance. In her eagerness to fight the fear of being alone she tried to convince herself that it was essential to behave as normally as possible. She was trying to breathe rather than drown. When she went out she always left a light on; when she returned and saw it shining behind the curtains, she despised herself for her ineffectual ruses. Inside once more, solitude burst on her like a gust of wind and there was only silence and darkness. It had always seemed to her that the dividing line between the sane and the insane was so fine as sometimes to appear indistinct.

She was afraid of falling into the snake pit. She was making mistakes and offending people. It was still too early. She was hurt by the insensitivity of couples overtly demonstrating their love for each other, the intimate glance exchanged, a kind of collusion above the heads of the crowd – the shared look that put the world back in focus – in spite of the raucous voices, the cigarette smoke and the whisky fumes. Whenever she found herself close to the happiness of others she felt her fall from joy most painfully. She would make her escape from a dinner long before the accepted time for polite departure, refusing offers of lifts.

One night later that summer she went to a dance in an extravagantly decorated marquee in the middle of Holland Park. She was dancing with a politician who was trying to be amusing while treading on her toes. The husband had been a good dancer; they had danced as one and even enjoyed showing off a little, aware of the admiration of others. Looking round at the sea of animated couples, she suddenly panicked, feeling as if she were stranded on an island. She had to escape. She made some inadequate excuse and rushed for the exit. Leaving the music and lights behind her, she ran and stumbled through the park, losing her bearings in the dark. As she fell and picked herself up, the giant trees surrounded her like demons. Shall I never find my way? Will I never break out? She was making for the sound of distant traffic. With her dress torn and soaking feet, she eventually found herself on a pavement. She had no coat or handbag.

'Do you need a cab?' A driver was pulling down his window. She sank wearily into the darkness and only came to her senses when the daughter opened her front door. They found some money to pay the driver.

CHAPTER 6

The politician who had taken her to the dance telephoned. 'What happened, are you all right? Everyone was worried about you.'

He came to see her, offering advice and comfort. 'You should have a purpose in life – a job that really interests you. What sort of work do you feel you would most want to do? Perhaps I could help in some way.'

'I'd like to do some interviewing.' The words came out without her having realized she had been thinking along those lines.

'Interviewing. What sort of people?' Before she could answer, he went on, 'I've got an idea. Why don't you travel round the Middle East – Kuwait, Abu Dhabi? The role of women is changing rapidly in that part of the world. It could be interesting. When I was Under-Secretary at the Foreign Office I spent some time travelling around there. I could give you some introductions.' For the first time for weeks she felt a flicker of enthusiasm.

She had never returned to the East since her Indian childhood. The husband had been many times on brief business visits but her memories of those early years were too precious and she had always promised herself that if ever she did return it wouldn't be for a mere fleeting glance. 'I used to speak Hindustani before I spoke English,' she said. 'I've forgotten most of it now. But I don't suppose it would be much help in the countries you're talking about. Anyway, would they accept a woman interviewer, a second-class citizen?'

'Well, it's a challenge, isn't it?' he replied. 'In any case, let's throw some balls in the air. I'm a great believer in plurality : put out lots of feelers and then if some come to nothing, you've always got the others floating. You'll be a great hit, I promise. They like blondes.'

These compliments and assurances of her ability to succeed gave her a disproportionate comfort. She realized that the grieving had brought with it a total lack of self-confidence. In her marriage, hardly a day had gone by without the husband praising her in some way – her looks, a new way of doing her hair, a special meal she'd prepared. She'd taken it all for granted, but it had become as necessary to her as breathing ; it was yet another prop which had been removed. She had been special in his eyes, therefore she was special. Now, what appeared to be a possible lifeline was being offered and she began to feel almost excited.

There had been other tentative suggestions from well-meaning people. 'Why don't you work for handicapped children? It would be worthwhile and rewarding, even if you only did it part time?' A worthy friend who ran a rehabili-tation centre for former drug-addicts rang her to ask if she would like to help. She recoiled from these proposals, feeling she was also handicapped and in need of rehabilitation. She knew all the arguments. By helping those less fortunate than herself, she would in fact be mending her own wounds. She was sure it worked for some, but knew she hadn't the necess-ary vocation or dedication. People in need who had crossed her path had always felt they could turn to her for help and support, and this she had given. But to work side by side with the sick and handicapped was beyond her. For several years she had been a magistrate in the juvenile courts and she was full of admiration for her colleagues who gave their services to the community in this way, but eventually she had resigned. She found the responsibility of passing sentence on young offenders too distressing, although occasionally her sympathies were with the police in trying to bring about justified convictions.

She talked over the Middle East plan with the daughter.

'Yes, you should go,' the daughter said, 'it'll do you good to do some work. But you won't go straight away, will you? It won't stop us going to Turkey?'

'No, of course not. It'll probably be in the New Year.'

Her friend had suggested they share the charter of a caique for two weeks at the end of the summer holidays and sail from Athens across to the western Turkish coast, ending at Rhodes. She had welcomed the plan as a further excuse to postpone making decisions about how to rebuild her life. Knowing virtually nothing about boats, she asked her cousin to join them. He was an expert navigator and sailor, and he had spent much of his life sailing single-handed across oceans. The daughter asked her closest friend from her old boarding school. To complete the party they invited an Italian painter who had just been abandoned by his wife and was living in London, a giant of a man, with a head taken straight off an ancient Roman coin – a Caligula with tight curly hair and sad brooding eyes.

When they gathered at London Airport for the flight to Athens, the mother was full of misgivings at the pot-pourri of people who would be living so closely for two weeks. But in her mood of self-absorption she could only be grateful for the haphazard quality of the adventure. Arriving at Piraeus Harbour they found the caique easily, wide mahogany bulwarks and twin masts towering above the sleek yachts and shiny floating motels. The Captain, a small dark-skinned man who looked like a quizzical bird, greeted them and introduced the crew. He came from Samos and spoke no English, but after a few days they developed a degree of communication. A see-saw motion of his hands denoted strong disapproval of anything ranging from Turkish officialdom to chic Patmos gays. Approval was a philosophical shrug of the shoulders, and an occasional and unexpected wave and cry of '*bazouki*' meant he was feeling gregarious. The crew consisted of a Greek cook, aged eighty-two, who always wore a grubby chef's hat at a rakish angle and spoke English with a strong Chicago accent, and the Captain's nephew, a good-looking young man with trendy side-burns who seemed to do everything from hoisting the sails, taking the helm and comprehending the vagaries of the outboard motor on the dinghy.

Everyone sorted themselves into the cramped space. The mother and her friend shared a cabin, while the painter and the cousin slept in the saloon. Later the girls opted to sleep on deck, which was also the Captain's favourite sleeping place.

The cousin, a strong-faced man in his early fifties, had never married. He was deeply religious and at his Catholic school had considered becoming a priest, but had decided he did not have a vocation. He had been a novice for a year before leaving to join the Navy during the Second World War. Her relationship with him had always been one of mutual trust and affection, but now she felt a deeper emotional dependence. The Captain respected him for his navigational skills and was persuaded to venture further along the Anatolian coast than on a normal charter.

As they sailed towards Turkey, they stopped briefly at Delos, Patmos and Samos. Life on board the caique left little time for thought. There were endless practical details to be coped with and the newness of the experience blunted the pain. It was only at night tossing in the narrow bunk that the demons encircled her once more.

They reached Delos, the birthplace of Apollo, in the evening, after the last tourist had left for the mainland. They wandered round the House of Dolphins and touched the huge marble lions and walked through the wild mint and rosemary growing in profusion amongst the ruins. Later, footweary but full of wonder, they swam back to the boat; her masts were silver splints in the full moon.

She began to feel the timeless quality of life on board. There were moments when past, present and future were the same. She longed for this nomadic life to continue forever. Sometimes the moods of the sea overwhelmed her, and she would lie on deck, letting the spray wash over her body, her mind empty. At Patmos they climbed for two hours up the narrow winding streets to the eleventh-century monastery, stopping halfway at the grotto where St John was said to have written *The Apocalypse*. The mother was not allowed to enter the monastery as her skirt was considered indecently short by the Holy Fathers, but the girls with their clinging jeans, decorated with symbols of sex and politics – 'Cure Virginity' and 'Babies against the Bomb' – and their seethrough T-shirts were allowed in to see the treasures. The cousin would have spent many happy hours pouring over the *Codex Porphysius*, the thirty-three leaves of St Mark's Gospel written in the fifth century on purple vellum, but the Captain was anxious to set sail for his home island of Samos, only a mile from Turkey. Famous as the birthplace of Pythagoras and for its good dry wine, Samos seemed to have a unique quality. The Captain insisted on playing host at the local night-spot. All the inhabitants were related to him, and ouzo and samos sec flowed while plates were filled with shish kebabs, zatziki and feta. They visited the Temple of Hera and saw a tiny chapel where the unconsecrated wine was stored in ketchup bottles. There was a sense of family that even she felt.

Their main goal was Ephesus. After many delays they cleared Turkish customs with the help of a good deal of whisky and cigarettes passing hands. They drove along the road which had been the old course of the Caystor River, down which St Paul had been rowed nineteen centuries before. Arriving at the Basilica of St John, they were besieged by small boys selling 'genuine' newly made antiques and postcards of phallic symbols. But nothing could mar the grandeur of the ancient city, and at the tiny House of the Virgin Mary they attended a service under the eucalyptus trees, the altar a slab of marble resting on two Corinthian pillars. Walking down the long marble Arcadian avenue and looking back at the vast amphitheatre, large enough to hold an audience of twenty-five thousand, she saw an emptiness far greater than her own.

Sailing by day and sometimes at night along the Anatolian coast, they explored many bays and harbours. Some had the unearthly quality of dreams. Every bay or headland carried signs or suggestions of the past. The girls were thrilled when a school of dolphins kept the boat company, leaping sometimes so high into the air they seemed ready to land on deck. They explored the tiny port of Kas with its lighthouse leaning precariously like a miniature Tower of Pisa. In the background were slender minarets covered with the intricate carving of Moslem artists, and round the quay crowded coffee houses, filled with men playing backgammon and Attaturk mahjong, overflowed into the streets. There they dined at a quayside café, feasting on kofte and raki served by a harassed Turk, his small son clutching at his trousers.

Maybe she had overdone the raki, for the next day she opted to stay on board when the rest of the party went to explore Kekova, said to be the most spectacular sight on the coast. At the last moment the painter said he would keep her company and do some work. He set up his easel at the stern of the caique and she climbed on to the top of the saloon hatch armed with sun-oil, cushions and a paperback by Doris Lessing. The sun beat down on to her brown back, and she automatically undid her bikini strap to avoid a white line. How strange it was that these small female vanities were beginning to reassert themselves. For months she hadn't cared about her appearance, she who had always been so meticulous about what her mother had called 'making the best of yourself'. She started reading but soon drifted into a troubled sleep. She was wakened by the painter at her side with a glass in his hand.

'I bring you some wine,' he said. She sat up, fastening her bikini. 'You know, you very beautiful woman – *veramente*. I watch you while you sleep. *Tu sei una madonna*.' She laughed with embarrassment.

'Don't be ridiculous – anything less like a madonna. . . .' But his gaze was sombre and slightly threatening. Oh God, he must fancy me. She realized she wasn't totally displeased, just amused. He was touching her arm with his fingertips.

'*Si, molta bella* – it is not right you are alone. You are made to be loved. Come, it is too hot up here. We will go to the cabin.' His lips were touching her shoulder while he pulled her towards him.

'No, I'm fine – please don't.' She pushed him gently away.

'But why? It will be good – you will see. You will – how you say? – live again.'

She laughed. 'Don't be ridiculous,' she repeated. 'We hardly know each other.' But part of her was imagining how it would feel to lie close to this male body and be desired once again. 'No, it's too soon.' She realized she was shouting, 'I don't love you. Please don't spoil everything.'

'Be calm, be calm – I only do what you want. Here, drink your wine. I will show you my painting.' He led her to the easel. 'What you think?' She looked at the geometric patterns in different degrees and shades of white, and then she looked beyond at the pretty white two-storey houses of Kas with tinted opaque windows. She narrowed her eyes and was aware of what he had translated into the language of abstract art.

'Yes, I like it,' she said truthfully. 'It's really good.'

'I give it you,' he said.

That evening before the party returned from Kekova, she went to her cabin and looked at herself in the tiny mirror. She was amazed at how little her face had changed. Although she felt a different being, those were the same features, the same hair. She put on some make-up and hunted for a pair of clean jeans and shirt among the pile of clothes in the drawer under the bunk, and tied a sash round her waist.

'You don't know what you've both missed,' they said on their return. The daughter looked at her intently. 'You seem different.'

'Better or worse?' the mother asked.

'Just different, somehow.'

The cousin was describing the underwater walls and tombs. 'Once a great Riviera – two miles of sunken quays – a lost mystery – an Atlantis. You should have come.' Their return journey to the caique in the dinghy had been dramatic, with the sea becoming rough and the waves breaking over the tiny boat. That night, sitting under the stars, sipping their raki, they agreed that this voyage had heightened all their senses. They had discovered the secret of adventure, the precariousness, the constant surprises of the Aegean, each hour taken on its own merit, its troubles and hopes wrapped within it, with no entanglements of before and afterwards to complicate such a simplified interval of time. They planned another voyage when they would explore further eastwards and follow where Alexander the Great had journeyed over two thousand years ago. Perhaps there was a future after all.

CHAPTER 7

That autumn the mother and daughter tried to work out a rough routine to their lives. The mother filled her days with physical activity, although unhappiness was still her total pre-occupation and she felt only a vague connection with the practical world. She was also finding it difficult being an ordinary citizen once again. The latter part of her marriage had been one of privilege, there had been people to take care of the mundane and time-consuming tasks of daily life. Now the endless forms and questionnaires poured in and had to be answered: sometimes she felt she would never come to the end of them. Letters from solicitors and accountants, forms from the Ministry of Labour and the Inland Revenue. In the past there had been secretaries and a chauffeur-driven car. Now she had to relearn about tube and bus routes. She preferred the buses, where she could lose herself in the outside world and listen to the jokes of the conductors and the repartee of the passengers. She found the tube somehow threatening, a race against time, and always the advertisements on the wall and alongside the escalators showing the endless couples – couples handing each other a drink, lighting each other's cigarettes. Couples, always couples.

She began planning her trip to the Middle East, visiting embassies for information and visas. Someone introduced her to a diplomat who had been *en poste* in Bahrain. He was full of advice and letters to people of influence, but she felt he was sceptical about the chances of success in her new role as a journalist. 'It takes time to gain their trust,' he warned. 'They will be charming and polite, but you'll find it difficult to pin them down.' Meanwhile she read everything she could find on the history and important figures in the Middle East, the sheiks and their advisers.

Her friends continued to include her in their social activities, and the painter telephoned her constantly to ask her out. She accepted everything and then, when the time came, regretted her impulsiveness. Before leaving the house she would make herself a strong drink to insulate herself from the pointlessness of the evening ahead. Her diary became full of engagements. There were some entries she had crossed out, events she and the husband had planned together, obligations to be fulfilled. As the Chairman of the corporation his life had been a ceaseless round of commitments and foreign travel, planned many months ahead. He had always tried to refuse any invitations from which she had been excluded. This month they would have been visiting Japan. She recalled their last trip to Tokyo and remembered how she hadn't really enjoyed it. 'How much easier it would be after a death,' she thought, 'just to edit out the unpleasant memories and prolong the good to produce an untruthful whole.' It was too tempting to summon up poignant episodes from the past, but she tried to push them to the recesses of her mind.

But in spite of her resolve, their whole life together was with her in every waking moment. She found she would be watching the clock at the time he would have been returning home from work, waiting for sound of the key in the lock. She remembered how she had quickly looked at the expression on his face for signs of his day's experience. Then the light kiss, the carefully prepared drinks, the flood of exchanges, the tiny rituals of a marriage. The luxury of sharing their day's disasters and, like children, keeping a minor success to the end. But the nights were still the worst when the sheer physical yearning would attack her suddenly and unexpectedly, like a treacherous intruder, and her senses became so acutely aware that sometimes she could even smell his presence. At these moments she felt she could never accept what had happened and was only pretending to endure. But there were other times when she found herself looking forward as well as back, and she clung to these tenuous moments of freedom that did not last.

The daughter was making a little progress at school and had begun to appreciate a more sophisticated approach to teaching. Her new school was run more on the lines of a university than the previous boarding school. The girls were given the responsibility to succeed or fail with guidance, but not dogmatic instruction.

'One of the most interesting girls in my form,' said the daughter, 'is really clever. She's a Communist. She has a habit of always dressing in grey. I really like her.' The mother had wondered at the gloomy clothes the daughter had been wearing lately, even borrowing one of her grey pleated skirts. 'We'd like to throw a party this term. Could we give it here?'

'Of course, darling.' She was relieved that at last the daughter had made a friend. 'Perhaps you'll ask her round and we'll talk about it.'

The following week the daughter brought her friend back to the house, obviously very much in awe of her. And no wonder. The girl had a quality of controlled vitality and great assurance, and was also exceedingly beautiful with large unblinking grey eyes, white skin and straight brown hair. Her clothes were all in different shades of grey. It turned out that she pursued her whims with a will of iron. She looked round the large L-shaped drawing-room, with its white sofas and yellow curtains.

'I suppose it'll do,' she said to the daughter, 'but of course, those will have to go.' She pointed to the pictures – the Matthew Smith, the Sutherland, the Frick lithograph. 'And I suppose we could cover the furniture with some Indian bedspreads or something to make it disappear.'

'Do you really think it's necessary to move all the pictures?' asked the mother tentatively.

'Oh yes, absolutely. I'll need to put up my posters.'

The daughter was looking nervous. 'Oh, that'll be easy,' she said.

'What about music, food and drink,' asked the mother, 'and how many people are you having?'

'We'll think about all that later,' they said, 'as long as there's plenty of red plonk.'

'Couldn't it be white? Red stains so.'

'Oh no, it must be red,' the beautiful girl said firmly.

As the day of the party approached the mother questioned the daughter about how things were going.

'Well, we've asked about twenty girls from school, but we don't know many boys.'

'It's not going to be much fun unless you ask some boys, especially as you want to dance.' She mentioned her friend's son who was in his last year at Eton. 'Why don't we ask him to come and bring a gang along?'

'I'll suggest it,' the daughter said, 'but I don't think she'll agree. She doesn't believe in public schools.'

In the end the mother took things into her own hands, and insisted. 'Just pretend they're from the local comprehensive.'

The boys from Eton came to the house on the morning of the party to arrange the music, carry all the pictures upstairs and move furniture. The mother worked all day peeling onions, cooking rice, making dishes of risotto and paella. About half an hour before the party was due to start, the beautiful Communist arrived, looking serene in an ankle-length grey silk dress. She put up enormous posters of Fidel Castro, Che Guevara, Lenin and Karl Marx, and flung some old Indian cotton bedspreads over the furniture.

'That's much better now,' she announced. 'And if we don't put the lights on but have a few candles, it will be quite passable. Where's the red wine?'

'I'm afraid I've only got white,' said the mother.

A slight flicker of annoyance crossed the beautiful pale face. 'Oh well, that'll have to do.'

How well the husband would have coped with this, she thought. They would have joked about it, and through the strength of his personality and humour he would have kept some authority over the young. He would not have been intimidated or wanted their approval; but she did.

The mother had asked her cousin to come along for support. He had always been particularly good with the young, but even he found it difficult to break through the generation barrier the girls had erected. It soon became obvious that the two of them were unwelcome and an embarrassment. Feeling like outcasts they shut themselves in the bedroom with some food and drinks. The teenagers started to congregate, and as more gatecrashers arrived the music was turned up louder and louder, and the screams and moans of the pop singers reverberated through the house. She lay on her bed, sipping white wine. The cousin, sprawling back on the silk-covered *chaise-longue*, had switched to whisky. As she listened to him, she thought how attractive he was and wondered again why he had never married. Sometimes he showed signs of some deep inner conflict as if he were waging a private war within himself. At these moments a muscle in his arm would twitch uncontrollably, and his eyes expressed suffering and some deep hurt which he would never allow himself to communicate. He was telling her of a book he had just reread – Huizinga's *Homo Ludens*.

'He tried to define the role of play in human culture. He would say there is an element of play in all religious ritual, just as there is an element of ritual in all sport – both being equally important to the human spirit, both essential to living – and defining us as *Homo sapiens* rather than ordinary mammal.' As she half listened to him and looked into those troubled intelligent eyes, at his square capable hands, she thought of the many months he had spent alone in his tiny sailing boat, pitting his body and mind against the elements, tossed by giant waves, battered by storms. In his faded corduroy suit, heavy-ribbed sweater and square leather shoes, she was acutely aware of his masculinity. I believe I could really love this man, she thought. The level in the bottle of whisky was going down and his voice was beginning to slur.

'And now with so much unemployment and early retirement people will have to be taught how to make the maximum use of their leisure – learn a craft. Malraux had the right idea. I read his *Anti-Memoirs* on the last Atlantic crossing, absolutely marvellous, it becomes a microcosm of the whole world I'd known. Here was this enormously cultured man of action who'd fought in the Spanish Civil War – a great Resistance hero and a great expert on Chinese and Cambodian culture. I found this mixture of commitment and culture so intensely engaging – '

The telephone rang. She looked at the clock – it was three in the morning. An irate neighbour was threatening to call the police. She went into the living-room and turned down the music. The room was in darkness except for the light of a single candle. All around her was the sickly smell of pot. She became aware of bodies everywhere, some clutching each other on sofas, some under tables, some swaying to the sound of the music and some with joints in their hands, gazing into space. Nobody took any notice of her, and she felt threatened and defenceless. She looked around for the daughter and found her on the sofa amongst a heap of bodies.

'The neighbours are complaining. You can't make so much noise or they're going to call the police.' The daughter followed her into the bedroom. Her face was flushed and the pupils of her eyes were dilated. There was a red mark on her neck.

'What's that?' asked the mother.

'Oh, for goodness sake, it's only a love-bite. And please don't spoil the party – we can't dance when it's as quiet as that.'

But the mother tried to be firm. 'You've got to, or I'll have to throw everyone out.'

At last things quietened. The cousin had finished the whisky, and she realized he couldn't possibly drive home.

'You'd better sleep in the spare room,' she said and led him upstairs. At the door he turned and held her for a moment in a clumsy embrace.

'Sorry I got a bit sloshed. Not much help I'm afraid.' She touched his lips and his roughened face with her fingers.

'You're always a great help,' she said. 'Sleep well.' Back in her bedroom, she locked the door and crept into bed where she lay, unable to sleep. She felt exhausted and rejected and allowed the tears of self-pity to flow as the music continued its relentless beat in the next room.

The next day the daughter slept until noon. She had dark rings under her eyes and was wearing a high-necked sweater to hide the mark on her neck.

'The party was a terrific success,' she said. 'Everyone said so.'

'I'm glad. How did your friend enjoy the Etonians?'

The daughter giggled. 'Well, really it was quite funny – she never discovered. She got off with some attractive Indian guy

43

and they've made a date. He didn't tell her he was a Maharajah's son and in Pop.' They both laughed.

The mother decided not to spoil the moment with talk of drugs : she put it off saying to herself, 'I'll think about that tomorrow.' Like Scarlett O'Hara, she had always been hopeless about facing up to unpleasant things and sometimes saw her life as a permanent in-tray, but she consoled herself that sometimes problems, if left long enough, went away of their own accord.

One decision she couldn't avoid was what to do about Christmas. In the past the family had always spent the holiday at the farm. She had thrown herself wholeheartedly into the preparations, pretending to complain, but really enjoying the last minute frenetic activities, decorating the tree, the feeling of relief when the tiny lights worked once again and the tattered top fairy was discovered amongst the tennis rackets. They had always driven to the country ahead of the husband. He would be working up to the last minute, do his shopping on Christmas Eve and fly himself down to join them in the evening. He would beg wrapping paper from the children and get them to help him. She still had the note he'd written on her last year's present. It just said, 'Darling, I can't wrap parcels but I love you even more than ever.' No, it wouldn't be the farm this year. She thought how public celebration hurt the lonely. Apart from going into retreat in a convent, escape was impossible. She had tried to include in the family circle anyone who was left alone, the spinster aunt, the child whose parents were abroad.

This year she would have liked to flee the country, but knew that she would try to create some sort of an occasion for the sake of the children. In the past she had got the pre-Christmas organization down to a fine art. Now every tiny errand and decision seemed to take on gigantic proportions. One day, shopping for crackers in Harrods, she again thought she was going mad. What did it matter whether she chose the red or the gold, the presents for all ages, or indoor fireworks with hats and mottoes, or useful trinkets and bad jokes? All around her people were filling up their baskets with confidence and determination. She knew she must decide – the shop assistant was growing impatient, sweat was breaking out all over her body. She thought she was going to faint.

'I'll come back tomorrow.' And she started running through the store. Outside it was raining on the long queues for the buses. She must have walked home. She couldn't remember.

In the end the friend came to her rescue with practical help and encouragement, and listened to her outpourings on the telephone late at night when sleep evaded her. They exchanged their worries over the drug scene, how tough a line they should take when they were told by their children that 'everyone is doing it' and their parents didn't mind. The friend came to lunch on Christmas Day and brought her son. They were joined by the cousin, the painter and the beautiful grey girl. The elder daughter had come down from university with her boyfriend. Presents were exchanged. The cousin gave her Illich's latest book on alternative education and the painter gave her a sexy black dress. The younger daughter wrote 'I love you more than anyone in the world' inside a copy of Ted Hughes's *Selected Poems*. As they sat round the old refectory table, she felt they had at least created some pretence of occasion. The son performed the ritual warming of the spoon over a flame before pouring brandy and setting it alight over the Christmas pudding, just as his father had done. They crossed arms and pulled crackers, put on paper hats and caught the end of the Queen's speech. Another hurdle over, she thought.

Later the daughter told her that none of them had felt like celebrating, but thought she would be upset if they didn't make an effort. The false faces we wear for the sake of convention, she thought, adults pretending for the sake of children and children for the sake of adults.

CHAPTER 8

In the New Year she and the cousin started to see each other more often. She would join him for lunch at a small Italian bistro near his office where he edited a nautical journal. The same waitress always looked after them – she had a vivid red birth-mark which covered the whole of the left-hand side of her face, but her eyes were beautiful and dark and she would gaze at the cousin with an expression of mixed admiration and defiance. Apparently unaware of her disfigurement, he would chat and joke with her before turning his attention to the menu.

As usual, when she was with him, life would momentarily be lived in the present, and she could focus on someone other than herself. His conversation was provocative and stimulating and she found herself turning to him more and more for advice about her life. She loved his clarity of vision, his naturalness and his disregard of convention. His views on every respect of life were his own conclusions, reached after much reading and inner searching for the truth. He was that most surprising contradiction, a totally good but unboring man. It was only when she tried to explore his emotional life that the shutters came down. His eyes became guarded and gently, but firmly, he changed the subject. She knew how deeply religious he was and wondered if perhaps he still regretted not becoming a priest. But, on the face of it, he appeared to enjoy his life. He had carved out a successful career as an expert oceanographer, writer and single-handed yachtsman who was admired and respected by the sailing community.

Although they had seen each other only intermittently over the years of her marriage, she knew her attraction to him was more than platonic. And now he appeared to be stepping into her life when she was most in need of male support and companionship. She had always preferred the company of men to women – she thought them less petty and parochial, with the exception of her one close woman friend. The conversation of women so often centred on domesticity, children, clothes and gossip.

One day, towards the end of January, as they were leaving the restaurant, he asked if she would like to spend the following weekend at his flat in Brighton. She said, 'There's nothing I'd rather do,' and meant it.

She walked home across Hyde Park, buttoning her coat tightly round her and pulling up the hood against the icy wind. She felt anticipation and excitement, and stood for a moment to watch the men and boys flying their kites by the Round Pond. As a girl she had cycled every weekday past this spot and across the Serpentine Bridge to her first job as secretary to a BBC producer. She had carried a radio in her basket and had listened to the latest pop tunes. During the summer months in her lunch hour she would often bring a book and a sandwich into the park and laze on the grass under one of the tall oak trees, enjoying the dual sensation of isolation and of community with the other Londoners around her. Now, in her insulated well of loneliness, she felt no sense of involvement with the kite flyers or the men steering their model boats by remote control across the pond. She no longer belonged to this city she had grown to love.

Her nomadic childhood in India had left no opportunity to put down roots. Her father, an Army doctor, was attached to no particular regiment, and so the family was always being posted to different stations. During her eight years in India she had vivid memories of a variety of places in which they had lived – a flat in the fort in Madras, a bungalow in Agra and another in Kanpur a few yards from the banks of the Ganges. But nowhere did they remain long enough to become part of the community. The father was also strict about not becoming overfond of possessions; she and her sister had been allowed to take from place to place only what each could pack into one small suitcase – anything over was given to the children of the Indian servants. But since she had grown up and lived in England, London had come to mean more to her than anywhere else. It had been different with the husband. He had felt a passionate love and loyalty to the Queen Anne house and estate in Bedfordshire of his boyhood, and his feeling had been transferred to the farm in Norfolk. He had had a deep belief in the permanence of the countryside, and planted belts of trees to be enjoyed by future generations.

She arranged for the daughter to spend the next weekend at the farm, and on Saturday morning she took the train to Brighton. The cousin met her in his battered *deux-chevaux* with its back seat full of sailing paraphernalia. They drove to his two-roomed flat on the ground floor of a Regency terrace overlooking the sea. The living-room, as compact as a ship's cabin, was furnished with the barest of necessities. It reminded her of a description she had read of Pushkin's cell; the only concessions to luxury were some pictures by David Jones and three shelves of books. A typewriter stood on a round table underneath the curtainless window and a painting on bark by an Australian aborigine hung over the settee.

Throughout the years she had known him, this was the first visit to his flat, and she felt an unusual barrier of shyness between them.

'I'd thought we'd lunch here,' he said, and from the corner

of the room which served as a kitchen he produced a bottle of red wine, a cooked chicken, some wholemeal bread and a tomato salad heavily laced with garlic and oil.

'Would you like it if we gave *Sorrento* an airing this afternoon? There's a good north-westerly and I'd like to try her with the new self-steering.'

'That would be great,' she said as she watched him set out the simple meal on the bare table. She thought, not for the first time, 'Why do men prepare meals so effortlessly? Plain simple food to satisfy hunger, not consuming time to titillate the appetite.' After Stilton and fruit, he made some strong coffee in a jug and fetched a box of Coronas from the cupboard.

'You're sure you won't?' She shook her head and watched as he carefully prodded the tip of the cigar with a match. 'I keep them for special occasions, like this,' he said. 'Your first visit.' She had given him the cigars for Christmas, a yearly ritual and a luxury that she knew he would never have afforded for himself. She got up.

'Do you mind if I . . .?'

'I'm sorry. It's just outside off the landing – French style. And here's the bedroom – I'll sleep on the sofa.' He put her Vuitton overnight bag on the single bed, the only furniture in the room, except for a narrow chest of drawers with a simple carved wooden cross hanging above it on the whitewashed wall.

'We'd better set off soon. You'll need this.' He threw her a large padded anorak. 'Might get a bit wet.'

Walking down to the Marina and across the intricate maze of jetties, he was stopped many times by members of the sailing fraternity, all with weatherbeaten faces and wearing the yachtsman's unofficial uniform of dark blue leather sneakers and oil-skins, some with peaked caps adorned with club badges. He was obviously a popular figure, and they talked about his boat as if they were discussing a mutual female friend. 'Thought she did beautifully in the Fastnet – not showing her age at all – no need for that face-lift yet.' 'Well, I'm not sure about that – probably have to invest in some new sails for her soon. Anyway, I'm trying this fancy self-steering gear on her today.' Edging *Sorrento* out of the harbour was no easy process. Unlike most of the other small yachts, she had no engine. They missed an elegant ketch by inches. He swore to himself and shouted at her to 'keep an eye on the fenders' as he steered skilfully with the help of the jib. In a few moments they had cleared the last boat and were rounding the harbour wall into the open sea. She tucked herself out of the way when he hoisted the mainsail, and began to relish the sensation of the cold, salty foam of the waves as they washed over the edge of the deck. Suddenly the boat tilted at a remarkably sharp angle, and she clutched the rail, pulling herself up as high as she could to escape the waves washing over the slanting deck. He turned round to look at her.

'You OK? Enjoying it? I'll take in a reef if you think we're going too fast.' She thought she'd never seen him so good-looking and relaxed as he manoeuvred his boat.

'No, I'm fine,' she said. Looking at him as he handled the wheel and sails with an almost tactile sensitivity, she knew suddenly and surely that she loved him. It was as simple as that. She wondered what it would be like to be touched by him in the way he was handling his beloved boat. And then she stopped thinking and started feeling exhilaration mixed with fear as they seemed to be sailing at right angles to the sea. She was revelling in the beauty and magnificence of the waves as they rose, curled and broke before them, and she was watching the scurrying grey clouds pierced by an occasional shaft of pale winter sunlight. She shifted her position to stop numbness, and he asked her if she would take the helm for a minute while he adjusted the self-steering. He showed her how to keep the sails filled on the wind and left her to cope as he disappeared into the tiny cockpit. The wheel seemed to have a will of its own as she strained to keep the boat steady. She saw an enormous wave approaching, and as it broke over the deck, she panicked and screamed for him to come back.

'Don't worry, you're doing fine.' But she was terrified and insisted. He laughed, but took the wheel from her. 'I think you've had enough. Just put your head down, we're going to go about.'

That evening he took her to his favourite pub – 'the only passable real beer around here' – and introduced her to his friends, mostly professors from the local university. Later they dined at a fish restaurant on the sea-front. They talked about his last Atlantic race and she asked him how much winning actually mattered.

'Well,' he answered, 'as Graham Greene said, "all failure is a kind of death", but, no – it's obviously fun to win races, but to me, just getting there, testing one's ability to survive, is enough.' He had had a traumatic experience when the boat upturned in a gale and was nearly dismasted, but his worst fears were those of a collision at night or of being becalmed.

'Once I was becalmed for days on end. I felt that the wind would never blow again and I'd remain in that particular patch of ocean forever. A pretty weird feeling.'

'And what about the fear of loneliness?' she asked.

'Surely everyone is alone, ultimately. Rilke, the German poet, said that to enjoy your loneliness you have to endure the pain it brings you.'

As they talked she looked into his unfathomable blue eyes and tried to understand the truth behind the words. For the first time since the husband's death she was beginning to feel that life might after all have a meaning again. He ordered brandies and more coffee, and later as they walked in step back to his flat, he took her hand in a tight hold. She undressed in the tiny bedroom and felt her body and face glowing from the exercise and sea air. Pulling on her dressing-gown, she walked into the other room. He was standing in front of the two-bar electric fire. Once again she was aware of constraint between them.

'That was the best day I've had for ages,' she said truthfully. 'I loved seeing you practising your craft.' He stepped towards her and took her awkwardly into his arms. As their lips touched, she felt a pure love between them, and a kiss of such sweetness that she wanted it to continue forever. She led him gently towards the small bare room, but he stood by the door and mumbled something about plans for the morning. A few moments later she heard the front door slam, the sound of him running down the steps, and she knew she was alone once more.

Travelling back to London in the Brighton Belle, she was overcome by shame and despair. How could she have so misread his feelings? Her body had cried out to him and been rejected. In the early hours of morning, after a night of tossing and turning until she had heard him stumbling back into the flat, she had eventually fallen into a troubled sleep. She had tried to behave lightly as if nothing unusual had passed between them. But after breakfast, she telephoned London for messages and pretended that the daughter had returned early from Norfolk, was unwell and needed her.

She looked round at the seedy elegance of the old railway carriage, with its solid mahogany woodwork and brass door handles, the white lace antimacassars with 'Pullman' embroidered in blue, the Victorian lamp with its scalloped dirty glass lampshade like a crinoline with frilled edges. Inset into the panelling opposite was a Japanese-style picture made of different types of wood. A cockney attendant, wearing a starched white monkey jacket, brought her tea in a Staffordshire china teacup patterned with blue and green leaves. But the swaying of the train made it impossible to drink without spilling half the contents on to the spotless white linen tablecloth. Subdued lighting behind panels of cut glass helped to create an atmosphere of safety, comfort and warmth. The steady rhythm of the wheels went de-dum, do-dum, de-dum and then, suddenly, do-de-du, do-de-dum, like an extra heart beat. The lamp, reflected in the window, raced past station after station and she realized she would soon be there.

Would life always be like this, a series of false starts and terrible errors of judgement?

At Victoria she went to a telephone box and dialled the painter's number. Would it be all right if she looked in for a drink? '*Naturalamente.* I am here, just painting. I wait for you.' She took a tube to Tower Hill Station and walked over Tower Bridge towards his studio on the south bank. Above her, improbable iron turrets, where princesses were locked away for ever. Behind her, the Tower in its fairytale gloom, where only Elizabeth I had ever come out alive after going in through the Traitor's Gate.

Her overnight bag weighed her down like chains. She dragged her feet.

The disembodied voice answered her ring.

'Good – you come. I think – she change her mind.' He was waiting at the door and took the bag. The room was long and narrow with a high ceiling and a large picture window overlooking the Thames and Tower Bridge. She walked over to the window.

'How beautiful. And all your pictures, they look so splendid here.'

He handed her a glass of champagne before guiding her round the studio to show her his work. On the easel was a large canvas with meticulously worked squares in different shades of white, the brush strokes in varying degrees of line and intensity.

'You remember?' he asked.

'Of course. Kas, the harbour.' He took the glass from her hand and led her to a thick white rug on a raised corner of the room.

'I think she never come – and now you are here.' He was looking fiercely into her eyes and started to undress her. She guided his hands and felt his insistent body close and wanting her. The need in her responded and they made passionate loveless love. In the distance the image of the White Tower became blurred by her tears of self-hatred.

CHAPTER 9

In the aeroplane to Kuwait, she looked through her notes. She had been given introductions to embassies and individuals and had planned a series of interviews. After the months of preparation she felt anxious to begin work. There had been so many frustrations; she had spent many hours waiting to see the Cultural Attachés of various Middle Eastern countries, who never seemed to be expecting her although appointments had been meticulously made. Everybody had appeared to be helpful, although slightly evasive. But now she was filled with optimism. A friend had written that a woman who was a leading figure in the Women's Movement in Kuwait would be interviewed, and she had another introduction to the Ruler of Abu Dhabi from the contact in the Foreign Office. Unfortunately, the timing was not ideal. The previous year a female journalist had insinuated her way into some male-only domains and had returned to the west to write lascivious and libellous articles, so that naturally the Arabs were suspicious of another woman interviewer.

But she desperately needed this venture to succeed, even in a modest way, in order to regain some vestige of confidence in her ability to create an independent life for herself. She thought back to her last futile emotional escapade and despised herself once again for using the painter's infatuation in an attempt to regain her femininity and deny her inadequacy. He had lunched at her home the next day in the small room overlooking the patio, once the children's nursery and now the most used room in the house. She bought taramasa-lata from the Pakistani shop across the street and made her own version of a Spanish omelette with onions, yellow, green and red peppers, fluffing up the eggs and popping it under the grill at the last moment so that it rose like a soufflé.

He had really talked about himself for the first time while they sipped their Frascati, and had told her about his life in Italy. His father ran a big computer company in Milan and he had quarrelled with his family when he had refused to go into business. He was married to an American psychologist, but they had decided to go their own ways. She had wanted a child, but he didn't believe in having children. 'Why add to the burden of overpopulation in the world?' And now his art was the only thing which really mattered to him. That and sex. Like other Italian men she had known, love was something apart, something given by the mother to her son and by the son to his mother, whom he put on a pedestal like the Virgin Mary. Sex was to do with procreation and enjoyment.

'Englishmen are too cold,' he said. 'They have no passion. You should have an affair. It would be – how you say? – a curing.'

'Like taking an aspirin,' she thought. She had always be-lieved in the unwritten law: never have an affair with a mar-ried man. And in her rare brief infidelities during her marriage, she had strictly adhered to it. Now, if for no other reason, she knew she would have to stop seeing him when she returned.

A stewardess touched her on the arm. 'Will you please fasten your seat-belt? We're about to land.'

Driving through the streets of Kuwait, she was disap-pointed by the towers of concrete buildings, the roads filled with noisy cars, the advertisements for prefabricated homes, cranes and concrete-mixers. She knew Kuwait was one of the more westernized of the Arab states, but she had also heard stories of desert picnics and hawking expeditions. Her imagination had taken her to carpeted tents where unspeakable delicacies were handed to her to eat by white-robed Arabs, their camels resting in the background under the date palms. The newly-built hotel was impersonal and she unpacked in the cold air-conditioned room with a feeling of dismay. She looked through a slit of a window at the silhouette of a dhow. The cousin had told her about them, beautifully-shaped handmade fishing boats. She had an urge to get a closer look, and wandered out to walk by the sea. After a few yards, cars started hooting at her and a man's leering face looked out and said something in Arabic. She realized she was the only female walking along the beach. She retraced her steps to the hotel and was followed by a crowd of laughing children. There was a message waiting for her. Najir would like her to go to her art gallery the following morning for coffee. She experienced a mixed feeling of anticipation and fear. So she wasn't in some kind of dream – something would happen. This would be her first interview, already set up in London. Najir Ohman had the reputation of being a unique and controversial figure in Kuwait. Not only did she own her gallery, specializing in modern art, but she was the first woman chosen to sit on the Board of the Arts Council which was part of the National Planning Board, a twelve-man think-tank, headed by the Prime Minister.

Entering the art gallery the next day, she had her first introduction to the ritual courtesies of the Middle East. Najir, wearing stylish western clothes, was younger and more attractive than she had expected. A vital, dark-haired woman in her mid-thirties, she fluttered about her like a delicate bird. A servant in flowing beige robes with a white head-piece held by a black cord, carried in a tray with an ornate silver pot. Sweet coffee was poured into tiny china cups and biscuits handed round.

'So you wish to interview me,' Najir said. 'I'm flattered but I don't think it will be of much interest in England. We're rather behind the times here, I'm afraid, but I expect you'd like to know something about the Harikanisaia, our Women's Movement?' After a few false starts with the recording machine and some faltering questions, Najir told of her crusade to liberate the women of Kuwait, nine in ten of whom were still veiled and illiterate.

'There's beginning to emerge in the Arab world a strong feeling for a movement which would involve women in the affairs of their country, particularly in education. You see, we live in a completely male culture – they're not used to dealing with women. But we're in a state of flux and the big issue is now not the veil but the Family Affairs Law, an archaic and medieval law which means that women are exploited by men and merely used as property. This is the law which oppresses the Arab woman the most. Everything else is becoming secular except this last issue. Marriages are still arranged – very few Kuwaiti girls marry outside the family – but it is just beginning. My mother and father were named for each other – they were first cousins, but had never met before. And the women lived in seclusion. They went outside the house twice: once for marriage and the second time for death. In Islamic law the man can obtain a divorce by simply saying, "I divorce you, I divorce you, I divorce you" in front of a witness and then it would be *haram* which means a sin for him to see her again without remarriage. But you see,' she added, 'our men have no concept of original sin, no guilt. I would say they are elegantly bisexual.' The telephone rang and Najir went to answer it.

Waiting, her thoughts started to wander. 'In Scotland they say divorce is death.' Not once during their occasionally turbulent marriage had the word divorce been mentioned. They had hurt each other deeply at times but, like the peeling of an onion, with each hurt and removal of a protective skin, they had reached a deeper understanding and love, until at the end. . . .

Najir had been speaking angrily on the telephone in Arabic, but she put down the receiver and went on, 'What I am fighting for is political rights for women.' To a tentative question, she answered, 'No, none of this conflicts with our religion. It is only the way the Koran is interpreted. In fact the first mystic was a woman and the first martyr was a woman. We are still totally ruled by males, but something is happening. It's like a bubble all through the Arab world, although we are still thinking in isolation. But maybe, one day. . . .' The recorder clicked to a stop.

She realized she had only brought one tape so she took notes as they continued to talk. She told Najir that her next stop was Abu Dhabi.

'My God, there you will find things even more backward. They make us look sophisticated.'

Back in the hotel she listened to the tape and blessed Najir for her unsuspecting contribution to these first faltering steps towards rehabilitation. She opened the half-bottle of vodka she had brought with her and drank a secret and silent toast to the future. She had doubts that she would ever be swept away by the mysteries of the East like the intrepid Isobel Burton and Jane Digby, but she was beginning to enjoy her own special adventure in Arabia, where women were also beginning to search for new identities.

Another vast concrete hotel with slits for windows as protection against the sandstorms from the desert; streets crowded with American cars and lorries spilling over with imported foreign workers. Pavements bustling with Arab men in long brown robes and occasionally a veiled and hooded woman. Abu Dhabi had been simply a palace fortress, two oases and a village. Since the oil had begun to flow, it had the largest per capita income in the world. It looked as if the monstrous towers of concrete had been put up haphazardly, without plans, askew. Everywhere were cranes and drills and half-completed prefabricated houses and a landscape of advertisements for material fulfilment.

Lying on her bed trying to reach people to make appointments, she was assailed by dismay and frustration. Everyone was polite, but time was irrelevant. '*Inshallah* a meeting may be arranged. I will call you back.' She had been promised an interview with Sheikh Zayed, the Ruler, through her contact at the Foreign Office. He would give her a decision after she had submitted her questions. In the meantime, the Sheikha Fatima would be delighted if she would take tea with her the following day at the palace. She had been told that although the Ruler had several younger wives, Sheikha Fatima was his first and favourite and the mother of his eldest son.

The next day a smiling young Egyptian girl from the Office of Tourism arrived to accompany her to the palace and to act as interpreter. They walked through the hibiscus-filled garden up steep steps and along marble corridors and were shown into the Throne Room. Unfurnished except for rows of chairs arranged round the walls, an ornate throne at the far end and vast chandeliers suspended from the ceiling, it gave the impression of a setting for an early Cecil B. de Mille movie. The Sheikha, a vast lady, her ample flesh tightly enveloped in scarlet silk, fluttered her arms as she chattered to the obsequious ladies around her. The usual hawklike leather mask hid her expression except for the eyes, heavily outlined in kohl, peering through the slits.

'There is a delegation from Kuwait,' the interpreter said. 'We will have to wait our turn.'

She was aware of a strong smell of incense, perhaps sandalwood, and trays of coffee and sweet cakes were constantly passed around. All the women seemed grossly overweight and giggled a great deal. The scene reminded her of an aviary of brightly-coloured twittering parakeets. Their arms were covered with bracelets and their fingernails beautifully manicured and painted – their only display of vanity. The minutes and hours passed slowly and she gazed at the enormous portrait of Sheikh Zayed hanging over the double doors at the far end of the long Throne Room. It was said that he had deposed his brother in a bloodless coup, but that he himself, under the influence of his mother Sheikha Salama, was peace-loving and a generous and just ruler, not hoarding money for himself but distributing it amongst his subjects. His compelling, fierce eyes set in a long fine-boned face, gazed out of the portrait, the only male presence. Suddenly the doors opened and a young boy of about fourteen appeared and waved to his mother. All the women quickly threw their veils over their masked faces and looked away. The boy laughed and waved again, but didn't enter the room.

As he ran off, her thoughts turned to her own son. He had been deeply upset at her display of violence in Norfolk when she had destroyed the portraits of her husband and herself. Later they had talked about it. She had tried to explain her motive, but he had failed to understand. She felt she, too, had thrown a veil over her face, a veil of grief, the mask of despair which had caused a rift between them. She realized that the bereavement had made her totally selfish. And withdrawn. She dragged herself once more into the present.

After what seemed like several hours, she was presented to Her Highness. More cakes were offered and this time she couldn't refuse.

'There is a friend of your country outside,' the Sheikha said, 'waiting to see the Ruler. His name is Sir Hugh Bousted; he has asked you to visit him at Al'Ain.' Sir Hugh Bousted was a soldier, author and traveller and one of Sheikh Zayed's earliest advisers. She had read his book, *Wind in the Morning*, and couldn't believe this piece of luck. Later, relieved to escape the gilded aviary, she saw him; a bowed, dignified figure in khaki waiting patiently in the shining corridor.

'I've been here six hours,' he said resignedly, 'but this is the Ruler's day for seeing his subjects. They sometimes wait all day for his *majlis* – he cannot bear to refuse anyone.' They arranged that she should visit him at his house in the desert the following day. He would send a Land Rover and his Indian driver. At last, perhaps, a real look at the sands of Araby.

After driving along a four-lane highway, they left the concrete town behind them and took the road to Al 'Ain. Gradually the road became a track. Now, all around them was the desert, undulating dunes with the sun beating down and casting vast moving shadows. She made desultory conversation with the driver. He had been with his master for many years and had often accompanied him on his travels. She told him she knew India, had been born there.

'Where do you come from?' she asked.

'It's not a place you would know,' he said, 'not a big place – a village called Kanpur on the bank of the river Ganges.' There seemed to be a blinding flash on the windscreen, as if it was on fire. For a second, she saw another fire: the fire that had terrified her as a child. She closed her eyes to shut it out.

'Memsahib all right?' She opened her eyes and saw the anxious expression on the driver's face in the mirror.

'Yes, it was nothing – it must be the heat.' But she was shaking with fear. She must pull herself together. She looked around her. The desert was even more incredible than she had imagined. An ocean of sand with ridges running across it like the waves of the sea and just as treacherous. Occasionally a herd of camels, led by a single Arab towards some well, would come into view, while Bedouin settlements sprang like occasional beehives out of the sand. The emptiness became a balm to her jangled nerves and before long her thoughts did abandon her, leaving an inner stillness and kind of peace. The relentless grandeur made her feel immensely small. Her personal grief and worries were insignificant, as relevant as a particle of sand in the desert. As the mountains of Oman appeared in the distance, they arrived at the hotel where Sir Hugh waited on the steps to meet them. They transferred to another Land Rover, specially constructed to drive over the rough terrain of his ranch. As they bumped across the craters and hills, he explained that Sheikh Zayed had given him his house on his retirement to look after his Arab stud.

'But,' he said sadly, 'His Highness is not so interested any more. An American breeder gave him a splendid black stallion and now he considers his own breed rather inferior.' He spoke about his life in nostalgic terms although he was loyal to the Ruler. But it seemed to her that he had been treated rather negligently. The previous night, after his wait of six hours, he had been told that an audience could not be granted. Yet he talked of Sheikh Zayed's compassion and love for his people, of the improvements that had come : free education, medicine and maintenance.

'He has what is known as *hazz* – good luck.' He laughed. 'That is considered to be the most important quality you can possess in these parts.' He showed her, with pride, the beautiful small Arab mares being exercised. They were made to gallop round a paddock encouraged by a gentle whip, as the sand filled the air around them. She and Sir Hugh ate a simple meal in the square white house where he lived alone, surrounded by books and photographs of the famous. In a central place of honour was a signed photograph of H E Sheikh Zayed bin Sultan al-Nahyan, Ruler of Abu Dhabi. 'This was his birthplace, you know.' Yes, she knew that, and she knew the Sheikh did not come here any more. That was the price of a life of service. Self-sacrifice was no way to forget, at least not for her.

CHAPTER 10

She returned to a host of minor problems which temporarily alleviated the major one. Her journey had been a failure – she had failed to get the interview promised by the Sheikh. Perhaps if she had waited a little longer she would have succeeded. At least she was interviewed on radio about the Women's Movement in the Middle East and had an article accepted by a magazine.

The daughter had crept back into her own shell and was uncommunicative. She looked thin and pale and had developed a skin complaint which would not respond to treatment in spite of visits to eminent dermatologists. As soon as she returned from school she retreated to her bedroom and lost herself in a book or played her stereo at a deafening volume. The room with its unmade bed looked like a corner of a refugee camp. In spite of entreaties from the mother to live a more disciplined life she announced that she preferred to live like that; and, no, she didn't think it was squalid and anyway, it was her life and her room and no one need bother about it. One day after she had gone to school the mother decided she could bear it no longer and, stepping through the piles of dirty clothes on the floor, tried to create a little cleanliness and order. Cigarettes had been squashed into half-empty coffee mugs. The wastepaper basket brimmed over with laddered tights. The dressing-table was littered with mascara, creams and ointments. Under the duvet was the woollen orange octopus which the daughter had had since she was a baby and had perversely grown to love. She straightened the duvet cover and gently replaced the octopus. But of course, the daughter was still just a baby – the spoilt baby of the family. Sorting out the mass of clothes to be washed the mother picked up a plastic bag with a small amount of some dark brown grains in the bottom. A feeling of panic engulfed her. Oh God, it couldn't be drugs. Perhaps it was only pot which was said to be moderately harmless. She was ashamed of her ignorance. She rushed to the telephone. The son had taken a degree in criminology and had studied the effects of drugs.

'Yes, it's very urgent,' she said. 'Can I see you today?'

'I have to make a speech at the House of Lords,' he replied. 'Meet me there for lunch.' They had regained their closeness without anything being said.

She drove her Honda through the entrance gates where the policeman on duty recognized her and let her park in the private car park. A top-hatted attendant guided her past the named coatstands and up the wide staircase. 'Thank you, I know my way,' she said. At the end of the long corridor she turned right into the Peers' Lobby, her high heels clattering on the Minton tiled floor. On her right were the solid brass doors leading to the Parliament Chamber and on her left the corridor to the Central Lobby and the House of Commons. In the dining-room festooned with tapestries, a waitress showed her to where the son was sitting. She recognized several people at nearby tables, a purple-robed bishop, an engaging peer who was constantly making controversial headlines by his habit of visiting notorious criminals, and some other familiar faces from the recent past. The son was obviously a popular figure. People stopped as they passed their table to congratulate him on a speech. 'Making quite a name for himself, this son of yours,' a member of the Conservative Party told her. 'Glad there aren't too many like him on that side of the House.'

After they had ordered from the unimaginative menu he asked her what the drama was all about. She told him of the party and her fears that a lot of the teenagers had been high on drugs, her worries over the daughter's moodiness and self-absorption and, finally, her discovery of the plastic bag in the bedroom.

'Have you got it with you?' he asked.

'Yes,' she said, touching her handbag.

'Let's have a look.'

'You mean here?'

'Why not? No one would expect us to be examining an illegal substance under the eyes of the Bishop.'

Surreptitiously she opened her bag and pushed the offending article towards him. He unwound the elastic band, bent down pretending to do up a shoe lace, and smelt it.

'I hope to God it's only pot,' she said, 'and not one of the hard drugs.'

His eyes were twinkling as he looked up. 'Coffee,' he said. 'She probably doesn't like the Nescafé at school.'

'Coffee – it can't be.'

'Well, that's exactly what it is.' A feeling, a mixture of relief and shame, flooded through her. 'Serves you right for being so suspicious.' He echoed her thoughts: 'Anyway, how are you?'

She told him of her trip to the Middle East, stressing the positive aspects, and her plans to do more journalistic work. They had always had an almost telepathic communication which made conversation virtually superfluous, and she knew he was thinking, 'Good, at last she's pulling herself together, no need to be so worried about her any more.'

'Grief seems to have released a residue of energy I never suspected I had,' she said.

'It's strange,' he agreed. 'I feel the same. Perhaps we all thought one dynamo in the family was enough.' He looked at his watch. 'It's nearly time for Prayers and Questions. If you want to hear my speech, we'd better go.' They waited for the Lord Chancellor and his entourage to make their stately procession through the Lobby. The Attendant called out, 'All remain silent and upstanding for the Lord Chancellor.' Bewigged, with the heavy gold mace carried in front of him, the train of his black robes held by an attendant dressed in velvet knickerbockers, the Lord Chancellor indeed made an impressive sight. She remembered the story of how on one occasion he had spied an American Senator whom he knew amongst the waiting crowd. 'Neal,' he had cried out in his booming barrister's voice and, as if responding to a Royal Command, the entire group had fallen on their knees.

Now she was seated in the small gallery reserved for the wives and widows of peers, while her son took his place on the Opposition benches. She looked round at the imposing chamber, full of familiar faces, where she had been before so many times – at the bronze statues of the barons who had forced King John to accept the Magna Carta, at the stained glass windows showing coats of arms of peers dating as far back as 1360. She remembered how nervous she had been for the husband. He had not been a good public speaker in spite of his natural gift for holding an audience with the strength of his personality and wit, so she was amazed by her son's self-confidence and at his polished performance. He was attacking the Government on their conservation policy and in particular on the agricultural policies which he believed were leading to the destruction of the natural habitat of wild life. In spite of interruptions and shouts of, 'Will the noble Lord give way?' from the Government benches, he held his own and sat down to discreet sounds from his own side of 'Hear, hear', and 'Well done'. As he had warned her that he would have to stay for the rest of the debate, she slipped out of the Chamber, down the red-carpeted corridors and out into the cold winter evening.

The daughter had already returned home and seemed less dispirited than usual.

'Thank you for doing my room, but honestly please don't bother again. I really don't feel the same way as you about it. Anyway, I've got something important to ask you. You see, I've been thinking – and I just think how wonderful it would be if you and I got a puppy.'

'Oh, darling. No, I couldn't possibly think of keeping a dog in London – all that exercising and everything.'

'Please. I promise I'll do everything. I'll take it for a walk before I go to school and when I get home. I promise it won't be any bother.' Her thoughts wandered while the daughter was talking. She had never particularly liked cats or dogs. They had always had Labradors at the farm, but she had not felt attached to any of them. In fact she had always thought it rather sad when people had pets to lavish affection upon because they had no human to love. Placing a bowl of food on the floor seemed an easy way to secure devotion. But how could she refuse? It might even break the barrier which had been growing between them.

They decided on a Dalmatian, perhaps because of the Disney film, perhaps because someone told them a Dalmatian was sweet-natured and easy to train; and they were going to have a dog and not a bitch. The son was full of light-hearted warnings. 'They're reckoned to be the stupidest animals on earth – and you'll never cope with all the exercising in London – and you should have a bitch, much more docile in spite of the snags.' But their minds were made up and, after looking at advertisements and checking out the names of Dalmatian breeders, one wet weekend they drove to Sussex. In a small suburban bungalow at the corner of a muddy lane they were shown a litter of puppies. The breeder went into details of the pedigrees and described the excellence and juxtaposition of the spots. She said they had first choice and held out one which she said was bound to win prizes.

The daughter was already holding a little bundle of black and white in her arms. 'Can we take this one? It is a boy, isn't it?'

'Yes, of course, but it's not the most perfect. I must point out, to be absolutely honest, he's got the smallest deformity in his tail.'

Sure enough, the tail which was wagging energetically had a tiny but definite bend in the middle.

'Oh you poor little thing,' said the daughter. 'We must have him.'

'Well, if you change your mind,' said the breeder, 'we'll always take him back. I never really can bear parting with my babies.'

In the weeks that followed mother and daughter were united in their absorption with the small spotted creature. They called him Zorba and forgave him all his misdemeanours. His basket was placed in the corner of the television room which had a door leading on to a small courtyard with flower beds, but unfortunately he was totally indifferent to the charms of the great outdoors and the floor had to be covered with plastic sheeting. For the first few weeks the daughter kept her promise and took him round the gardens in front of the house before and after school. But the routine soon lost its attraction and the mother found herself joining the world of people whose lives are governed by the needs of a member of the canine world.

'No, I'm afraid we can't come for the weekend – you see we've got this dog and no one to leave him with.'

'Do you mind if we walk while we chat – he hasn't had any exercise today.'

In spite of her reservations she realized she had succumbed to the demands of a small four-legged creature.

One week the cousin telephoned and asked if he could stay for a few days. He appeared unaware that anything had changed between them, and they didn't allude to the Brighton episode. A male presence in the house was a comfort to both mother and daughter and she enjoyed the ritual of preparing the evening meal for the three of them. Later when the daughter had gone to bed, they would talk until late into the night: she curled up in front of the fire; he, opposite, a glass of whisky in his hand, telling her of an article which had impressed him in the *TLS* or the *Tablet* or about the book he had been asked to write about his sailing experiences. Whenever the conversation became too personal he would gently steer her away leaving her with a sense of loneliness and inadequacy. The awareness of his physical presence dominated her utterly. She told the friend of her innermost feelings and received in return a warning that she was merely trying to replace her loss with unreal solutions.

Gradually a pattern emerged. Whenever the cousin had work to do in London he would stay in the spare room which had been her son's. Soon they took his presence for granted.

One night she went to a dinner party. They had all been friends of the husband from the world of politics and business. The man provided for her was an Ambassador whose wife was visiting Paris for the collections. While listening and trying to contribute to the pompous and artificial conversation, something inside her seemed to explode – she longed to leap up and rush from the room. The careful cosmetic faces of the women, their smart fashionable dresses, the preserved conventions to hide real emotions, the platitudes and complacent attitudes of the men. The Ambassador was turning to her.

'I suppose you'll get married again very soon – people who were happily married once always do.'

Arriving back at the house in a state of hysteria she looked up to see if the light in the spare room was still on. It was. She rushed upstairs and found the cousin in bed reading. She sat on the edge of the bed and tried to explain the futility of the evening. He put his arm round her.

'Do you want to stay here?' he said. 'I promise I won't touch you.'

CHAPTER 11

She woke the next morning feeling that the prison bars were closing even more tightly around her. All her efforts to lead a normal life seemed to have failed. 'Perhaps I need proper medical help,' she thought. She telephoned the friend.

'Before taking that step,' the friend said, 'would you think of joining me on a course of Insight?'

'What on earth's that?'

'Well, it's a movement started by an American. Less fierce than EST – but it teaches you to come closer to your reality, a means of self-development, not just cerebral but through the whole being. It's meant to help you express more strength, more joy, more aliveness, and move beyond the layer of illusion and games that mask the pain, anger and resentment blocking us from experiencing our reality.'

'You sound as if you're reading their blurb.'

'I was. But honestly, why not give it a try? We'll do it together. Only five days intensive training. Anyway, think it over.'

She lay back in the bed. She had always been sceptical when American friends had told her of their sessions on the couch, and of the various group cults. Her colonial and Protestant upbringing had disciplined her to be stoic about mental and physical pain, so why now wallow in the therapeutic luxury of sharing her innermost thoughts and fears with total strangers? Well, perhaps for once she should try what she found most difficult. Perhaps it was time to discard the mask, remove the sticking plaster and start to face the reality of life alone even if it meant allowing the blood to flow.

The fifty hours of experience called Insight took place in a London hotel and started on a Wednesday evening, lasted for three evenings, two full days and Saturday and Sunday from half-past nine to midnight. She and the friend arrived together feeling as if they were children again on the first day of school. The atmosphere was in fact more like a business seminar. They were handed badges with their Christian names printed on them. She looked around the room for any familiar faces and luckily recognized no one. There was a slight predominance of women, ages varying from twenty to sixty-five. From the background came a catchy tune which was to announce the beginning of every session. They sat in rows while the leader introduced himself and spoke with an almost childlike conviction. 'When we discard our beliefs and prejudices about what we think we should be and come to what is, that's when we will find that love, joy and beauty, that essence, spirit and energy inside of us.'

He was a short, plump man with a halo of golden hair and didn't give the impression of great intellect or any quality of spirituality. 'All of you have all this inside of you before you even take Insight. Maybe you have covered it so you don't recognize it. We are here to help you uncover it.'

He then introduced the other American trainers and helpers. She felt how young they all looked and was reminded of those identikit dolls that come with clip-on clothes. They were all men of medium height, with trim figures: beige knife-edged trousers, navy blue blazers, striped ties, short hair and expressionless eyes. The ground rules were being explained by one of the lookalike dolls, a good-looking young man sitting on a raised platform, demonstrating points with his arms, reminiscent of a perky young schoolmaster. The rules were written on an enormous blackboard and they had to promise faithfully to obey them or 'leave right now'.

Rule 1 was not to divulge certain things which happened during the course, as an element of surprise was an important factor.

2 Don't play Trainer.

3 Don't smoke or take drugs.

4 Don't talk to anyone about what has happened during the day.

5 Be punctual.

6 Don't reveal any confidence.

7 Obey the Ground Rules.

8 Don't do anything that radically changes your life until at least two weeks after the training.

He told them they could join in as much or as little as they felt inclined, but stressed they would regret not having participated fully as the training progressed.

She glanced at the friend who was looking decidedly sceptical. 'I suppose now we're here we'd better plunge right in,' she said.

The first lesson concerned posture. 'How many of you are sitting with your arms or legs or both crossed?' Guiltily she uncrossed her legs. 'Don't you realize that by sitting like that you aren't allowing the natural flow of energy to run through your bodies?'

Now for the first exercise. 'I want you to choose a partner. It must be a complete stranger.'

Immediate panic – like a terrifying party, she thought. Now don't go for the tall attractive man, she might get a brush-off. Avoid the sad dejected lady looking even more nervous than she felt, she might be stuck with her for ever. Compromise – a fairly friendly-faced man approached her.

'Stand facing your partner maintaining eye-to-eye contact.' Help again! Like those games children play : 'I bet I can stare at you without blinking longer than you can stare at me.' But this was a different sort of game. They were there to learn some fundamental truths about life and themselves.

'Now, in turn, ask three questions of your partner. One: do you feel you could be completely open with me? Two: do you feel that you could be partially open with me? Three: couldn't you be open with me at all? Remember to keep eye-to-eye contact.'

Again panic, and her first rejection. He told her he could only be partially open with her.

'Now your partner must ask you the same questions.'

Cowardly, she said she could be completely open. Why not? She had nothing to lose and she didn't even know him.

That first night she got into bed feeling drained, but nothing compared to the total exhaustion she was to feel later in the course. The daughter was full of curiosity.

'But why can't you tell me all about it?'

'It's one of the Ground Rules. I promised.'

'I think it sounds silly – just like school, and you're even paying for it. How much *are* you paying, by the way?' Guiltily she reduced the figure by half. 'Well, anyway, I think it's a ridiculous waste of money.'

The following days and various exercises blurred in her mind, but as the time went by she became aware of the atmosphere of accumulated pain in the large darkened room. The anonymous faces soon acquired identities and the level of intelligence was high. Friendships began to form. The sessions went on sometimes after midnight with only short breaks for lunch and coffee. At one early session there was an ugly example of mass hysteria when the trainer was thought to have treated one of the participants unfairly. He wrote on a white sheet pinned to the blackboard: '*Your trainer is unfair.*'

'Anything else?'

'It's all too banal,' someone shouted. He wrote it down.

'Why do you all wear the same clothes?'

'*I don't like his clothes.*' Aggression was in the air as he wrote with the expression of a martyr: '*Self-satisfied, arrogant, too American.*' She hadn't shouted, but had been in sympathy with some of the attackers and guiltily saw that when he turned to face them, he had tears in his eyes.

The most difficult moment came for her during an exercise connected with pain. 'How many of you are in either mental or physical pain? More or less all of you. OK. So how would it be if you got rid of that pain? Would anyone care to come up here and take part in a demonstration?' A girl went up. 'So, where is your pain?'

'Sort of here.' She pointed vaguely to her stomach.

'Well, why don't you take it out and look at it? Just imagine you've got this thing. Now take it out. What shape is it?' She made a vague gesture.

'What substance?'

'Kind of slimy.'

'Now, feel the shape of the substance.'

They all had to do the exercise and gradually people's pain seemed to diminish into small tiny things and eventually disappear. 'But surely it's not possible,' she thought, 'to get rid of pain this way, by pulling it out of you, feeling it and destroying it.' How many around her were pretending? How strong was the motive to please and be applauded?

One of the more exacting exercises involved sitting face to face with a partner and asking certain specific questions about their childhood. Each in turn had to be first the mother and then the child. She was asked if her mother had always been there when she most needed her. Her mind went back to a night in India when she had wandered from her bed on the veranda of their bungalow and seen a sight of such self-inflicted torture, a sight she thought she had erased from her memory forever. Now the memory and the terror returned, she was sobbing like a child and the 'mother' was holding her in her arms. She was not alone. Many people broke down during this exercise: young people who had been estranged from their mother or father and felt deeply disturbed and unhappy, parents who had lost contact with their children. They all said they would make an effort to repair the damage.

But the meditation session she found the most rewarding. The trainer stressed that Insight was not only cerebral, but spiritual. 'It teaches you that you cannot understand the motivation of life through the mind alone, but it is necessary to look at ourselves through several levels of awareness at once to have a sense of detachment from life's game of snakes and ladders; to learn to concentrate on our strength rather than weakness.'

She had had lessons in yoga meditation before and found she could detach her mind from her body in quite a short time, drifting outside herself to achieve a sense of floating in space, emptying her mind by concentration and achieving a trance-like state of self-hypnosis. She emerged from these sessions with a sense of having been in a dreamless sleep, although, in fact, she had only been semi-conscious for a matter of minutes.

The doubts she had about the course were pushed into the back of her mind while she battled with fatigue. The effort to try and keep an open mind throughout the five days left her emotionally and physically drained.

On the last day they were told to form two circles, one inside the other. By each circle moving in opposite directions, everyone eventually faced everyone in the room, looked into their eyes and were told they could embrace, hold hands or just pass on. The close proximity and the emotional pressure had released a torrent of love and nearly everyone embraced. One young girl broke down in hysterics. 'It's too much, no one has loved me before. I don't know what's happening – I can't cope.' She had to be walked up and down while she calmed herself. Finally it was truth time. They were asked to say, if they wished, what, if anything, Insight had done for them as a group. One eminent writer said : 'All my life I've been able to communicate through my pen or to give lectures but I've never been able to communicate on a personal level. I could never have believed that in five days this could be achieved.' As he sat down he was crying unashamedly.

Driving home that last night she tried to comprehend the experience. It had certainly reconfirmed her own reserve and her gift for hiding it, her inordinate fear of rejection, her curiosity about her fellow creatures. A mass of contradictions. But what about any basic truths about life? Of course, if people could rid themselves of their prejudices and hate, and reach out to total strangers with love, this would mean that evils of crime, violence, injustice and war would cease. An Utopian world. But surely getting to know, trust and love another human being must necessarily be a slow process and therefore all the more rewarding. Wasn't there something unreal about instant friendship – and instant enlightenment – and instantly reliving all the past? As she wearily pulled the bedclothes around her she said to herself, 'I'll think about it tomorrow. . . .'

PART TWO

When I was a child, I understood as a child. I thought as a child; but when I became a [woman], I put away childish things.

1 Corinthians 13:1

Hesse said that the most important thing we had was remembering, but the second most important thing was forgetting.

CHAPTER 12

There are many things I think I have forgotten, but they come back to me, and they are me. Perhaps to know the truth about myself and face the future, I have to return to the beginning, look through the glass clearly, then face to face.

My mother was the second youngest in a family of eight brothers and sisters. Their name was Dunbar and they were of Scottish descent. Her father was in 'Railways' and when she was twenty-five, he was in charge of Welsh Railways. At that time they lived in a large gloomy house in Cardiff. She longed to escape from her restrictive, puritanical family background, and trained as a nurse. Her eldest brother also went into Railways ending his career as head of the British-run Sudanese Railway, where he also became a well-known Egyptologist and archaeologist and wrote a learned book called *The Rock Painting of Lower Nubia*.

My mother got her first job nursing at a children's hospital in Edinburgh. Her best friend there happened to send a photograph of her to a medical student brother in Ireland. The student, later my father, was the youngest of ten children who were descended from a line of the Montrose Scottish Protestants called Graham. The family had settled in Dublin in the eighteenth century and had lived there ever since. His father had been Senior Wrangler at Cambridge, where his five elder brothers were sent. But money was scarce and, when it came to my father, he had to settle for Trinity and a degree in medicine. He was known as 'Rags', for the simple reason that by the time his elder brothers' clothes had been passed down to him, that was how they looked. He had an aunt who had been a missionary in China, where she had been murdered, and a great-grandfather who had been Napoleon's doctor on St Helena. I have a miniature of him painted at the time. All six brothers went either into the Church or into medicine. One, Uncle Togo, became a famous specialist in Dublin. Another, Uncle Chris, was Senior Chaplain to the British Navy, very worldly and made a lot of money on the Stock Exchange. When he officiated at my wedding at St Paul's, Knightsbridge, he complained to the family that he'd never been paid for it.

My father was considered a bit of a tearaway when he was young and very attractive to the opposite sex. He specialized in gynaecology but never particularly enjoyed being a doctor. I think he was intelligent enough to know that, in those days, there were not many ailments a doctor could cure. It was before antibiotics, and quinine and aspirin were the only important medicines in use. He used to hand out harmless coloured pills to his patients saying that these would cure them. My mother always said he had a great bedside manner, adding rather bitterly, 'I wish he'd use it more at home.' As a medical student he had experimented with hypnosis, which had cured him of a severe stammer. He and another student made various experiments on each other and once he cut a vein in his hand to see what would happen. One of his favourite tricks was to show us the broken vein wriggling like a worm across the back of his hand. He could also make wonderful shadow pictures of wild animals on the wall.

Anyway, when he qualified, he joined the Royal Army Medical Corps and was immediately posted to India. He decided to take a wife with him, and when he received the photograph of his sister's friend, he went to visit her in Edinburgh. It was a whirlwind romance and in the wedding photograph they made a handsome couple with his brother officers holding an arch of swords over their heads.

My mother was very attractive, small, dark with a perfect complexion and laughing brown eyes. My father was over six feet, thin, fair-haired with pale blue eyes, a high forehead and sensuous mouth.

For the honeymoon they went to Istanbul, where apparently I was conceived, and then on to India via the Middle East, probably to stay with my archaeologist uncle. There my father had a curious adventure. A certain sheikh heard of his power of hypnosis and wished to be cured of insomnia. My father was summoned and, through an interpreter, hypnotized the sheikh into a coma. The guards became highly disturbed and, thinking their master was dead, started threatening my father with swords. The interpreter having disappeared, my father thought he would meet a nasty and premature death. Fortunately the man reappeared in the nick of time, the sheikh was awakened and the story had a happy ending.

My father was always strict with my younger sister and me during the eight years we were all together in India; he had hoped for boys and treated us as if we were. I came in for the harshest punishment because I was the naughtier. My sister, Bunty, was delicate and said to be 'a bit difficult', with a tendency to fly into tantrums particularly if she was made to wear a pretty dress to a children's party. My parents sometimes found her impossible to manage, but she and I were very close and it was usually left to me to persuade her into obedience. 'You cope with her, Sonia.'

I had my own methods – usually bribery. 'If you do so and so, I promise I'll wake terribly early tomorrow so that we can see our ponies lying down asleep in the stables.' It was always a mystery to us that we never saw them sleeping.

Once, when I was about three, I undid a packet of cigarettes and gave her all the tobacco to eat in her cot. This resulted in several whacks of the ivory hairbrushes that were kept on top of my father's chest of drawers and used either to give hundred strokes to my long hair or a few hard smacks on th bottom. One day I decided I didn't like the white plaster o our room and persuaded Bunty that, if we got enough bottle of ink, we could paint it black. I received a very sore botton that time. But I loved my father as he was a fount of knowl edge and he would never disappoint me. If he didn't know th answer, he would go to his *Pears Cyclopaedia* and look it up He was a great believer in *Pears Cyclopaedia*, and the soap.

I was also fascinated by his little office, where he did hi experiments and where he kept his pickled snakes and scor pions in bottles. What he did with them I shall never know but he was always writing articles for the *British Medical Jour nal*, so perhaps he was contributing to medical knowledge i some obscure way.

He also had a valuable collection of stamps, and he and used to spend hours sticking them into albums, while h would tell me about the various countries. I think this firs lesson in geography is what produced my love of travelling

When I was old enough, he would put me on the handle bars of his bicycle and take me to the military hospital, whe he did his daily rounds. He would be wearing his khaki short and tunic with his Sam Browne shining across his chest and we'd both be in our hard white topees. They made a great fus of me at the hospital and I think it was my first awareness o the real India outside the military compound around ou bungalow. I still remember the sick Indians lying in thei beds, their eyes lighting up at my father's approach. The truly believed he had the magical powers of a modern witcl doctor. I remember the beggars we passed on the road and my father explaining to me how their parents mutilated then on purpose to secure an income. But I was told on no accoun to give them money as I would be surrounded by hundreds o others. I once disobeyed him when I saw a creature dragging himself along on his stumps on the path outside our veranda, and immediately the bungalow was besieged. I never owned up, so was spared the hairbrushes.

When our *sais* took us riding every morning after *chota-hasri*, my father would put rupee coins between our knees and the saddle to make us grip properly and we had to show they were still there on our return. Although he couldn't afford to keep his own polo ponies, he was a keen player. One Christmas he had special miniature polo sticks made so that we could learn the game.

He used to read us stories by his favourite author, Rudyard Kipling, and I came to know many of them by heart. My mother loved poetry, particularly Rupert Brooke. I think she must have started secretly pining for the English fields, and honey for tea. But she also read all the English classics and our only early education came from reading, which we did avidly. Later a spinster aunt came to stay and somehow we acquired a basic education of sorts. Aunty Doll was a gentle, serious person, self-contained and deeply religious. My mother was always trying to 'get her off' and eventually a tea planter did actually propose marriage. My aunt turned him down, her reason being that she didn't think she could really stand the climate. But her gentleness was deceptive; at times she was resourceful and on one occasion extremely cour- ageous. It happened when my parents were away. She was in sole charge of the bungalow, when suddenly we heard a weird howling in the trees at the edge of the compound. Anid, the bearer, came rushing on to the veranda screaming, 'Memsahib, mad jackal. Very dangerous.' The howling came nearer and Anid started to shout at us to run away. 'Go inside immediately,' said Aunty Doll in the firm tone she used when not to be disobeyed. From the window we watched as she pulled down one of my father's rifles from the rack on the wall, loaded it and stood her ground as the wild animal advanced. The next thing we knew was that a shot had been fired and the jackal lay dead a few yards from the steps of the veranda. Aunty Doll stood very still, red in the face and shaking violently. She had never fired a gun before in her life.

At eight years old, white children were meant to leave India as it was considered dangerous to their health to stay on. Parents had to make a difficult choice: either to remain together and send their children to boarding schools 'at home' or to separate, the mother travelling with the children to stay with them. I didn't think that for my mother it was going to be a difficult decision. She always seemed rather afraid of my father. Although not conscious of it at the time, I don't think their sex life was particularly satisfactory. I remember once – the wall between their room and ours must have been rather thin – her crying out as if in pain, 'Please, Rags, don't', and then the noise of sobbing. But she adored us children and possibly because of his harshness, used to spoil us behind his back. Little things remain in my mind. Whenever they went to a party or ball, there was always a present under our pillows when we woke up – a sweet or a dance card with a tassled pencil. Once, when we had been shut up in our room on a diet of bread and water, she crept in with a plate of fish and chips. We lived mainly on curry and rice and, as Bunty hated curry, my father said she must just eat the rice. When my mother objected, he said, 'All the Indians do, why shouldn't she?' But sometimes for a treat at supper we would have our favourite meal – fried fish, chips and tomato ketchup – and I have loved it ever since.

How did we look? Bunty was very thin with enormous brown eyes and dark hair. Although later she grew into a beauty and was often taken for Elizabeth Taylor, as a child she was almost plain. Physically brave, she was painfully shy particularly of men. If ever there was what she called 'Man' in a room, she would refuse to enter.

I was equally thin, with very long legs, blue eyes and curly blonde hair. I had slightly protruding teeth – even putting quinine on my thumb hadn't stopped me sucking it – and when my mother tried to persuade my father to get the dentist to fit me with a brace, he refused. 'A waste of money and pure vanity. Use an elastic band, quite good enough.'

He had no time for female vanity. Even when he gave us our vaccinations he put them in a prominent place on our legs which left large unsightly marks. I remember my mother crying for hours.

CHAPTER 13

Looking back, it seems that so much of life was full of drama and danger. Travelling by train seemed to me the height of adventure. We were always hearing stories of trains being derailed, delayed or damaged by violent landslides. Sometimes journeys lasted over three days, which meant we would see a lot of our parents as our *ayah* and the bearer would have to travel in a different part of the train. I loved the bustle of the crowded stations with Indians selling their wares to us through the carriage windows. I loved the beauty of the landscape as we wound round precipitous mountains and over raging torrents. I loved the nights when the imagination could fly to the sound of the wheels and all dreams seemed possible. There was always the feeling that something extraordinarily exciting might happen and often it did. Once when my father had stepped down to the platform to buy something, he didn't reappear. As the train started to leave, my mother was screaming out of the window, 'Rags, where are you? Hurry up.' But there was no sign of him. We were terrified and thought we had lost him for ever. My mother immediately pulled the communication cord. After an age and much discussion in Hindustani with the guard, the train slowly started to go backwards. Eventually we were back at the station to find my father waiting on the platform calmly smoking a cigarette. Apparently an Indian had collapsed with a heart-attack and my father had revived him with heart massage and organized an ambulance to take him to hospital.

But day-to-day living in those times was full of dangers. Apart from snakes, we went in fear of scorpions and always had to wear shoes. As a warning of what would happen if we were stung we were shown people whose legs had swollen to enormous proportions. One week, before the rains came, the compound outside the bungalow became infested by cockroaches and it looked like a pink sea of moving creatures. My father, wearing his high leather riding boots, put us on his shoulders and carried us through, pretending to drop us and catching us again. He had that sort of sense of humour. Once in Madras, when we were living in part of the Fort, before I could swim, he took me on his back into the breakers where people were surfing. I had heard there were sharks in the sea. When he threw me up in the air and just caught me in time, I was petrified with fear. I still am afraid at the sight of large breakers. If anyone I love goes in them, I worry until they come back.

My mother used to adore going to parties and giving them herself. But she was very insecure socially, which sometimes made her appear snobbish. The bearer was always being made to look into the box at the bottom of our drive to see if anyone had left their visiting card. If a boy came round with a chit from the Colonel's wife inviting them to drinks, it was a moment of great satisfaction. Chits were their only means of communication – a single sheet of paper with a message written on one side, folded in half, one corner turned over and the name written on the outside. When my mother gave a dinner, I always loved seeing the table laid out with all the best glass and silver, and then going into the cooking quarters in the special area behind the bungalow to see the cooks prepare the food, some of which they did with their feet as well as their hands. I don't think my mother ever saw meals being prepared; she would just give the menu to the bearer.

So much of life took place on the veranda. In the evenings, when my father had finished work, they would sip their chota pegs and gin-and-its. I think that's what gave my mother a liking for gin in later years, but she didn't drink much when she was young. We would be allowed by our *ayah* to join them before going to bed, otherwise we didn't see much of our parents. Sometimes carpet-wallahs used to come and spread one rug after another on the veranda for our inspection. My father became quite a connoisseur and after much bargaining would occasionally make a purchase.

Bunty and I were looked after by a series of *ayahs*. One in particular was quite cruel, but I think we were too frightened of her to tell our parents, and they never knew what she put us through. I loved knitting and was halfway through a dress for my china doll, Rosebud, when she decided I must finish it before I could go to bed. I knitted for hours into the night, tears mingling with the wool. One night, when she was still very young, my sister did the unmentionable in her bed and *ayah* made me get up and wash the sheets in the tub. *Ayah* was very ugly and always chewing red betel. We slept on the veranda under mosquito nets, and the only time *ayah* forgot to tie the net under Bunty's cot my parents arrived back late from a dance just in time to see a snake climbing into the cot. My father rushed for his gun and shot it dead. I expect he pickled it later. He was a very good shot and sometimes went on tiger shoots. I still have a faded snapshot of me clad in jodhpurs and topee standing on a large dead tiger with my father, rifle in hand, standing proudly at its side. Pig-sticking was another of his favourite sports, and he would often join his fellow officers in trips up country.

In Kanpur we had a bearer who, for some reason, was sometimes left in charge of us. He used to make me sit with him under a rug and feel his thing. I just thought it a bit odd and boring, and eventually he would get up and pee milky stuff in front of me. I never said anything, but his little game must have been discovered because he was sacked. Later I saw him leering at me in the bazaar, but he did not come near me.

Going to the bazaar was a big treat. It was like going to the circus with all the monkeys for sale, stalls full of brightly-coloured glass bangles, and the snake charmers. We would stand transfixed as the snakes rose and swayed from their baskets to the sound of the flutes.

Once, on our way to Agra, where my sister had been born and which was a favourite place of my father, we ran over a large cobra in the road. It made the car give quite a lurch. My father was thrilled. As the cobra was too big to pickle, he had the skin made into handbags for us which lasted for years. I remember the disappointment when he first took me round the Taj Mahal, finding nothing inside it but a lot of empty rooms, though I did think it romantic that a man should build a vast monument to the memory of his wife.

At an early age I was conscious of my femininity and my effect on the opposite sex. I was what my mother called 'the darling of the Regiment'. I can remember a good-looking subaltern stopping outside our bungalow, looking down at me from his enormous black horse and tapping me lightly with his cane. 'Here, my beauty, I've got a bone to pick with you. You cut me at the polo ground yesterday. I was most upset.'

It was my first introduction to grown-up teasing. Pick my bones, cut, what did he mean? I didn't even have a knife. But I pretended to understand and smiled shyly.

The first time I fell in love was at the age of seven with a boy called Peter. For his eighth birthday his parents gave an enormous party, inviting children and their parents from up to a hundred miles away. Even for India, that was quite a distance. They must have been in a grand regiment or rich or both, because it was the most sumptuous party I'd ever been to. It all took place in tents in the grounds in front of the bungalow. First we were told to go into the biggest tent. At the far end there was an enormous rainbow with hundreds of bags of gold coins at its foot. We all took one and were told we could spend them in all the other tents. Some had puppet shows, some snake charmers, some toys for sale. I bought two goldfish in a bowl. Then there were games, which the boy Peter thought were very silly. We played one where we were divided into two rows and skipped towards each other singing. Peter was between me and a little Indian Princess. Suddenly, she cried out, 'You're holding my hand too tightly – I don't like it.' I remember a feeling of violent jealousy. I told Peter he could hold my hand as hard as he liked.

After the game, he took me off to show me his birthday presents, one of which was a bicycle, but he said he wished it had been a motorbike like his elder brother's. He asked if I'd like a ride on the motorbike. In a minute we were hurtling through the tents, and all the parents came out of the bunga-low and started screaming because he was completely out of control and couldn't stop. I remember loving it and hanging on to him very tightly. Eventually the elder brother saved the day by grabbing hold of the handlebars. Going home in the car was a tricky business, all that way along bumpy roads trying to keep some water in the goldfish bowl. I don't think I ever saw Peter again, but it was the first time I remember feel-ing both jealousy and sexual attraction.

Another children's party was given by the Viceroy for one of his elephants' hundredth birthday. My mother was very excited because we were going there and made us especially pretty dresses. She made all our clothes and most of her own. My sister refused to wear her dress and there was nearly an ugly scene until I promised I would give her my second mongoose if she did. Anyway she was fonder of animals than I was and much preferred them to people. We had to queue up for rides on the old elephant at the Viceroy's party, but it was very friendly and knelt down for our *ayah* to put us in the

little house on its back. It was very wobbly getting up and we
all screamed with delight.

Yet the event which made most impression on me as a child in
India happened before I was eight, when we were living in the
bungalow at Kanpur close to the Ganges. We slept on the side
veranda which faced on to the road leading down to the river.
We didn't have a fence round the compound but instead had
several watchmen patrolling with rifles. Often at night
funeral processions used to pass which were very colourful
affairs. Four men would carry the body on a bier which
would be decorated with bright silk and flowers. Hundreds
of relations and friends would surround it, chanting songs
and covering it with gifts and coins. There would be a stream
of beggars in the rear picking up anything that fell on to the
road. Our *ayah* told us that they would take the body to the
Holy River to place it in the water together with the food,
money and clothing necessary for the journey to Heaven. In
this part of India, the *ayah* said, the people believed that the
River was their God.

One night something different seemed to be happening.
The person being carried on a sort of platform wasn't dead.
She was a young woman dressed all in white with flowers in
her hair. She was completely still, praying to herself. I
thought it must be a wedding, so, as our *ayah* was fast asleep,
I decided to follow the procession. I slipped past the night
watchmen and kept a short way behind the small crowd of
people. They stopped before they came to the river. But
where was the bridegroom? Suddenly I realized there was no
bridegroom, but the body of a dead man. I was by this time
rigid with fear, but I couldn't move. The woman stood in
front of the body and raised her arms. Other women gave her
bunches of flowers. She took them and raised them above her
head and then gave them back, turning round in a complete

circle as she did so. She kissed the dead body and then, one by one, took off her rings. Some people were building a big bonfire and, when it was burning furiously, the woman was tied to a sort of scaffolding and taken towards it. I wanted to run away, but was transfixed as in a nightmare. The woman looked as if she were in a trance and there was music, and all the people were singing and shouting with joy. Suddenly there was a terrible scream, and I found I was running, cutting my feet on the stones, tearing my nightdress on the trees, until I reached the veranda. I rushed to our *ayah* and started sobbing. 'Oh dear child,' she wailed, 'you've seen *suttee*.'

CHAPTER 14

As we pressed against the rail on the deck of the P & O troop-ship taking us to England and waved to my father standing on the fast-disappearing jetty, I felt an emptiness in the pit of my tummy. He stood very upright in his khaki uniform, his white topee showing over the heads of the crowd and he lifted his cane to us in a final salute. I was eight years old and Bunty five. 'Don't cry,' my mother said, 'I'm taking you home.' But mixed with the emptiness was rage. This was our home and we were deserting my father; how could my mother do this to him?

It must have been a difficult journey for her. The three of us shared a cabin and it was a rough voyage, which in those days took six weeks. Bunty was seasick most of the time and I was sulky, withdrawn and full of resentment against my mother. I refused to play with the other children on board and spent most of the time hiding behind one of the life-buoys on the top deck, either buried in a book or watching critically the antics of the passengers. Deck quoits was the popular game and one day I saw my mother playing with animation and obviously enjoying herself. She looked very pretty in a white dress with a red sash and her dark brown eyes flashed with a liveliness that was new to me. Her partner was a young offi-cer I didn't know. As the days went by I started following her stealthily, keeping my distance. As always on board ship, the passengers were beginning to divide into groups, but my mother's group seemed to be the most active. They played bridge, deck games, drank, danced, and my mother's partner was always the same young officer.

'Why don't you go and play with the other children?' she asked in desperation one day as she saw me lying behind my life-buoy.

I gave her what I hoped was a deeply disapproving look. 'Because I don't feel like playing and never will again.'

'I can't understand it,' I heard her say to her new friend. 'She has never been tiresome like this before.'

During the daytime I never recalled the terrible incident I had witnessed by the banks of the Ganges, but in the course of the voyage I suffered from nightmares and would wake up sobbing and sweating with fear. My mother would take me in her arms and comfort me, believing that it was the separation from my father that was the cause of my tears. I didn't disillusion her, hoping it might add to her guilt.

One night, a few days before we were due to arrive in England, there was to be a fancy dress ball. My mother decided to go as a gypsy. For days beforehand our cabin was strewn with curtain rings being sewn on to coloured scarves and a fringed bedspread was miraculously transformed into a twirling skirt. My fury knew no bounds as I watched her giggling with self-appreciation as she made up her face in front of the tiny mirror. 'Well, what do you think, girls?' Bunty, still looking faintly green, murmured her approval and I remained scowling and silent. 'Oh, you are a spoilsport, Sonia.' But she didn't really care about our reaction as she dashed from the cabin. While the throbbing music filled the ship and the hours slipped slowly by, my resentment grew until I could stand it no longer. My cotton nightdress was trailing to the ground as I crept out leaving Bunty asleep. I reached the crowded saloon and soon spotted my mother dancing in the arms of my enemy. Couples parted in alarm as I rushed towards her. 'Come away, you must come away.

How can you be dancing when Daddy is all alone in India?'
My mother, deeply embarrassed and upset, pulled me by the
arm out of the saloon and back to our cabin. My job done, I
was soon fast asleep. Whether she returned to the dance, I
never knew. I have no further memories of that journey but,
thinking back, I feel sorry for my mother. It was probably the
first time she had enjoyed herself for years and God knows
what my father was getting up to in India.

My mother had always been vague, but I had never realized
quite how vague until, as the gangplank was lowered at
Southampton, I asked, 'Where are we going to stay?'

'Oh, I expect we'll find some digs somewhere.'

'But which town?' I asked.

She looked a little embarrassed. 'Well, I hadn't really
thought. Perhaps we'll just stay here for a while until we
decide what to do.'

After a friendly taxi driver had loaded our luggage, she
asked if he knew of a good small hotel or guest house. 'As
near to the sea as possible,' I added. I think I felt that being
able to see the sea I would somehow feel closer to my father.

Everywhere we tried was booked up, but eventually we
found someone who was prepared to find some room for us.
Our digs were on the front and consisted of a living-room
with a small kitchen at one end, a bathroom and one bedroom
with a double and a single bed.

My memory of the months we spent at Southampton is decidedly hazy except for two events. The first occurred a few
days after our arrival. Rummaging amongst my mother's
possessions in the desk – I was always a very nosy child – I
came across a small snapshot of the officer she had flirted with
on board ship. I was overcome with such a violent fit of jealousy that I tore it into as many pieces as possible and scattered them all over the floor. My mother was most upset
when she discovered them. 'You silly girl, he was only a
friend. What on earth's the matter with you?' I suppose it

was jealousy once removed on behalf of my father. I only know it is one of the fiercest and basest of emotions, and impossible to control.

The other memory was when I discovered that my mother had only half the second finger of her left hand. When I asked her about it she turned scarlet and said she had lost it in an accident with a mangle when she was a girl. She had always been clever at hiding it and when she played bridge she always held a pretty chiffon handkerchief in her left hand. When I told Bunty about it, she was horrified and refused to share the double bed with my mother for several nights. My father later told me that she had even hidden it from him until years after they were married. How sad to be ashamed of so small a deformity.

The next thing I recall is that we were living in a flat in Worthing. My mother's parents had retired there after leaving 'the Railways' and were living with Aunty Doll, who had returned from India a year before with no regrets in spite of her rejected tea-planter. Money was extremely short, and to pay for the fees of our day school, my mother took a job in a children's hospital. She had odd ideas of economy. She still made all our clothes, and Bunty and I were always well-dressed; when I met someone years later who was at the same school, she said that one of her earliest memories was of me in a smart belted camelhair coat. But loo paper was considered a luxury and we had to make do with newspaper brought back from the hospital. Her ideas on morality were also ambivalent. Certain items of 'Railways' cutlery seemed to find their way to the flat as did towels marked 'Worthing General Hospital'. But if either of us said or repeated an unkind word about anyone, we would be severely ticked off. Punishment was a thing of the past, and the ivory hairbrushes became a distant memory, as did my father.

We didn't seem to have many friends. There was a red-headed boy, the son of one of my mother's bridge four, who told me he was going to be a famous photographer and who would make me sit for hours in different poses and then wait in his dark-room while he developed his masterpieces. But I didn't like him much and was always trying to avoid accepting invitations to his house. My mother considered his family rather grand and tried to encourage our friendship. 'You must make an effort, Sonia, pull your weight in life and keep your end up. Not just for your sake but for Bunty, too,' adding mysteriously, 'I don't want you to go through what I did as a girl.' I was to hear this theme repeated all too often in the years to come. Bunty was being just as difficult as ever and hated the day school so much that it was thought that a small local weekly boarding school might be the answer. This was to prove a mistake and every Sunday evening when she was due to return, there would be terrible scenes which went on until my mother's soft heart weakened and she was allowed to stay at home.

Bunty was my only confidante and I would pour out to her everything of interest that happened to me. She was a willing listener and sat silently looking at me with her large brown eyes staring from her pale face. She enjoyed living vicariously the life that she was too frightened and too shy to live herself. I would tell her about the red-haired boy and about the man who always followed me back from school. When no one was looking, he would undo his trousers and pull out his thing and show it to me. I never thought of telling my mother as, even then, I had a subconscious knowledge that she needed protecting from the unpleasant side of life. She should only be told good news, never anything bad.

Suddenly our fortunes changed. My father had been posted home and was to be Head Medical Officer of the Duke of York's Cadet School at Dover. We found ourselves in a large furnished Victorian house from which we could see Dover Castle. We had a maid and my mother felt it was almost like being back in India. We were sent as day girls to a convent in the town, but both Bunty and I disliked the nuns intensely. Apart from one who always seemed to be in as much trouble as the pupils and was performing constant acts of penance, the nuns appeared to us as a sadistic group of black crows. We were endlessly being punished for some minor misdemeanour and were either doing seven compulsory runs round the playground or writing out a hundred times, 'I must show more respect for Mother Superior.'

One day I conceived a plan that we would run away to the Castle to frighten everyone, including our parents, and show how miserable we were. Food and water were smuggled to school in satchels and during morning break we made our escape. We had been to the Castle before, in a group, and more or less knew our way around. The first day we spent happily exploring the drawbridges, moat and dungeons. Although I was the leader, Bunty was the braver and would always take the first leap across a ditch into the unknown beyond. Of course, we had no idea how cold and miserable it would become during the night, but, when Bunty implored me to return, I stubbornly refused and insisted on sticking it out. In fact it was a great relief when we were discovered the following day by a search party sent out by our frantic and worried parents. My father's fury knew no bounds. We were too old for beating, but were banished to our room for three days on a diet of bread and water and no books. Naturally, my mother smuggled up extra rations and my copy of *Gone With The Wind*, which I managed to read by torchlight under the bedclothes. It turned out to be a happy end to our adventure, though a failure of our trial of strength. We were immediately dispatched back to the convent.

It was at Dover that we heard Neville Chamberlain's announcement on the radio that German armed forces had invaded Polish territory and, as a consequence, we were now in a state of war with Germany. My father immediately joined the British Expeditionary Force. He would soon leave for the field hospitals of France to take part in what was to be known as the Phony War. I was being sent to the Royal School at Bath, a semi-charitable institution for the children of poor Army officers, where the fees were subsidized but the education was said to be excellent. My mother said she couldn't stand the thought of returning to Worthing, but would take a flat in London. She later found one off Cromwell Road, where she worked in a club for Polish officers by day and as an air raid warden by night. Bunty was to go to a small boarding school where she, at last, seemed fairly happy. The idea was that she would eventually join me at Bath, if I didn't find the life there too Spartan for her.

CHAPTER 15

The Royal School for Daughters of Officers of the Army was certainly Spartan and I was soon writing to my parents that on no account should they submit Bunty to such an ordeal; she wouldn't stand it for twenty-four hours. It was run on Army lines and the discipline was ferocious. I shall never forget the first day, sitting at the long refectory table for tea and having to eat unrefined bread without butter or jam. With our knowledge of diet now, we would all be consuming it dutifully, but then it seemed awful. The girl sitting next to me said she would throw up if she had to eat it. I managed to smuggle out her piece of bread under the elastic of my navy blue woollen knickers. She subsequently became my best friend until, later in my school career, I deserted her for the large spotty-faced captain of lacrosse, on whom I'd had a crush for some time.

Over our knickers and white woollen vests, we wore cream Viyella shirts, the striped school tie and dark blue pleated gymslips tied at the waist by a cotton sash. After we had been at school a year, we were allowed to change into mufti on Sunday evenings. We still used certain Army expressions and slang, and were all very conscious of our military backgrounds.

'What regiment is your father in?' asked the girl in the bed next to mine in the dormitory that first night.

'He's in the RAMC,' I answered proudly.

'What on earth is that? Oh, you mean he's just a doctor.'

I blushed violently, which was something I did until late in my teens, and then I foolishly asked what her father's regiment was.

'Oh, he's in the Green Jackets,' she replied.

I soon realized there was just as much snobbery amongst the girls about their fathers' regiments as among the officers themselves. It had never occurred to me that my father wasn't a member of one of the noblest of professions and that the Army was lucky to have him. I still kept this belief fiercely to myself, but didn't dare announce it publicly in case of ridicule. That night I cried silently into my pillow.

The school was on top of a hill overlooking the splendid city of Bath, but, as far as I can remember, we were never shown the beautiful crescents or the Roman baths. But I do remember the Abbey where we went every Sunday, and the man falling off Jacob's ladder on the façade. It seemed to me that I had fallen off a ladder into an enormous, dark, damp prison from which I would never escape. Visiting the school years later, it appeared to be a rather pleasant, not very large building with a good view over the city. It only proves how our memories can play tricks on us, especially when we are miserable.

In our case, however, we were to have a lucky reprieve. The Marquess of Bath, who was one of the Governors of the school, offered his home, Longleat, to the authorities for the duration of the war so that we could escape Hitler's bombs. We were to go there the following term.

The great long galleries were turned into dormitories, temporary huts were built in the garden for classrooms and we were allowed the use of the magnificent grounds. I can't say that we girls really appreciated our surroundings, but they were certainly an improvement on Bath. I remember the labyrinth of stone chimneys and statues on the lead roof, the great staircase, and the family portraits looking down on our

rows of narrow beds. Some of the atmosphere must have
seeped into our subconscious minds, but I don't believe at the
time we were fully aware that we were at a boarding school in
one of the most historic Elizabethan mansions in England. I
came to know and love the grounds and the descending lakes
designed by Capability Brown. We were allowed to ride and
I was able to escape by myself and roam with my pony
through the woods and fields, jumping the fallen trees. The
days at Longleat seemed to be forever sunny with hours spent
lying in the long grass, sucking the juice from the broken
stalks and reading, reading, reading. Of course, my favourite
hero was Heathcliffe and, as I hugged my hot-water bottle
close to me in bed at night, my erotic fancies knew no
bounds. I would one day be loved by a tall, dark, brooding
man who would put me through every kind of torment until I
eventually won his love. Actually hot-water bottles were essential, as there was no heating in the house except for the
enormous log fire in the hall. We had jugs of cold water and
basins in which to wash ourselves in the dormitories, and
these were constantly spilling and spoiling the ceilings below.

Lord Bath, an old-world figure with his high, white wing
collar and formal clothes, still lived in the house and used to
appear at Speech Days, sitting on the platform with our Head
Mistress. I remember him best standing on the top of the
steps at Longleat, flanked by his enormous Great Danes. We
all adored him and I'm sure our Head Mistress was in love
with him.

I was lazy at school, or so said my reports. I know I never
did much work until just before exams, when I crammed like
mad and just managed to pass the vital grades. But I was good
at games, a demon with the lacrosse stick – 'Cradle, girls,
cradle,' sang out the beloved spotty captain – which I must
say hasn't helped me greatly up the ladder of life. Nor did
becoming captain of cricket promote my chance of future
employment, although I was a demon fast bowler. Winning

the long jump and high jump, however, and being clapped by my friends' parents, gave me a taste for audience appreciation which was probably a dubious asset. But I excelled in one sphere which has certainly enhanced my life, and that was in drama. I was quite a good actress, but a better director, which is what I enjoyed doing most. Putting on the school play or pageant at the end of term was a thrill unlike any other I'd known. Unfortunately, my parents never seemed to be in the audience.

My father was with the Army in France and my mother was working in London. The one time I do remember her appearing at school I would rather forget. It was at the time of my confirmation and I was passing through a deeply holy phase and taking my religious instruction extremely seriously. I couldn't wait for the confirmation ceremony and first communion, which was to be conducted by the Bishop of Bath and Wells. I love Wells Cathedral with its great curving stone x's holding up the central spire, and the medieval clock with its revolving figures and the small Lucifer-like creature of Jack Blandifer striking the bell on the hour. My mother had promised to attend, but wasn't among the other parents who had congregated for a glass of sweet sherry before boarding the coach with us. I was bitterly disappointed, but just as we were halfway down the long tree-lined avenue, a small lady was spotted running after us waving a book. Much to my deep shame it was my mother, carrying an ivory-covered prayer book, a gift from Aunty Doll. The coach was stopped and she joined the rest of the parents. My poor mother, she always let me down at the most important moments in my life.

During the holidays my father appeared on leave in London. The war had taken its toll of him. Three years earlier he had been involved in the evacuation from Dunkirk. As the doctors had to stay on the beaches until the end to see their wounded safely on to the boats, they took the fiercest shelling. He was also torpedoed twice on the short journey home across the Channel and had been on sick leave for months before returning to the fighting. At the end of the war he was invalided out of the Army and suffered from bouts of illness until his death at the age of sixty-seven. During our brief reunion I persuaded him that if I could pass my School Certificate a year earlier than the normal age of sixteen, I should be allowed to leave school. He accepted the idea, having always disliked paying the school fees and being impatient for me to start earning my own living. My higher education was to be learnt by living my life.

I was a year younger than the average age in my form, so, although lazy, I must have been somewhat precocious. That year at Longleat, I decided to apply myself to work and gained my School Certificate at the age of fifteen. In my final report the Head Mistress wrote, 'Sonia has a good brain and should do well in life if she doesn't decide to become a social butterfly.'

My mother's grand friend in Worthing had told her that the chicest secretarial college was called Queen's and was at a place called Englefield Green, near Eton. This appealed to my mother's snobbery and, as my father was abroad fighting in the final stages of the war, he was unable to voice his disapproval. By taking an extra job in London and making endless personal sacrifices, she scraped together the fees to send me for a year's finishing at Queen's. Apart from acquiring the necessary qualifications as a secretary, we learnt bookkeeping, a foreign language of our choice, housekeeping and flower arrangement. As we increased our speeds at shorthand and our fingers flew over the keys of our typewriters to imaginative phrases like 'Now is the time to come to the aid of the party', our minds plotted trips to Eton and parties in London.

I shared a room with the daughter of an Earl who had never before left the stately home where she had been privately educated and protected from everyday life. She was an exquisite, shy, doll-like creature with a porcelain complexion who was terrified of the rough world in which she now found herself. I became fascinated by her, she was so vulnerable and mystified by the everyday things around her. I was also fascinated by the way she folded her sweaters, carefully turning in the sleeves and then rolling them into long sausage shapes. Apparently, that was how her lady's maid folded them. In turn, she was amazed by my practical worldliness and we became bosom friends. When I first took her to London to my mother's flat, she was terrified of the city and admitted to me that she had never crossed a main road by herself before.

Our flat became her second home and later, when she was ordered by her parents to join the WRNS, she used to appear looking immaculate in her Able Seawoman's uniform. But I trembled to think of how working in a barracks at Portsmouth contrasted with her previous existence.

Most of my contemporaries at the secretarial college had gone into one of the Services or the Foreign Office, but I decided to apply for a job as an assistant to a BBC producer. We put out a programme for hospitals called *Here's Wishing You Well Again* and I was sometimes allowed to introduce the stars. At home we were shorter of money than ever and I took an evening job working in a watch factory. We would sit on benches in front of an enormous moving conveyor belt and place our tiny pieces of metal in the appropriate spots. I quite enjoyed it as a part-time job and can never go along completely with those who raise their hands in horror at the monotony and soul-destroying quality of factory work. Of course, it is mindless and there is no job satisfaction, but there is a comradeship, my thoughts were free to wander and there was the consolation of a pay packet at the end of the week.

The war in Europe was drawing to a close and the young men who took us out dancing in various clubs like The 400 were old for their years. They had seen too many of their contemporaries maimed or killed. Although they were still only boys, their eyes were those of old men. When they were on leave from the front they crammed every moment with pleasure and the girls lucky enough to be working in London were not short of escorts or admirers. As my mother was still working at the Polish Club, there was at the flat always plenty of drink, which she sometimes took in lieu of salary: my mother's time spent in India drinking chota pegs on the veranda had given her a taste for gin. In later years I had to persuade her to change to whisky, which made her more benign. This was after there had been several disasters when she started falling about and breaking bones. She also smoked heavily and on two occasions set her bed alight. But while she still had us with her she kept herself under control. She was a great favourite with my boyfriends and they loved her for her generosity and for the light-hearted atmosphere she created. But she was very puritanical and always insisted on staying awake until I returned from a party or a nightclub, and I had to pop into her room for a final kiss.

There wasn't the pressure in those days for girls to sleep with the man with whom they were having a flirtation. It seemed we were much more romantic. Although as sexually aware as the present generation, we were all told that our virginity was something precious to be preserved for 'the real thing'. In my mother's eyes, 'the real thing' was any eligible young man, preferably with a title, who proposed to me. She was longing to 'get me off'. It is not being conceited to say that proposals were fairly frequent; I think the young men who had experienced the horrors of war longed to establish a permanent relationship as soon as the war ended. My new friend's brother had fallen in love with me. He was stationed at Portsmouth in the Navy and we used to gather at my mother's flat before going out on the town. If the bombs started, we went straight to The 400, which became our air raid shelter. My mother was over the moon that I had the chance of marrying into one of the grandest families in England and was furious when I told her I had refused him. A few months later he died tragically when he fell into a manhole in Portsmouth dockyard, and some members of his family blamed me for what they felt had been suicide. It was the first time in my life that someone close to me had died. It seemed impossible to comprehend that a boy so young and carefree should have his life suddenly ended. How could I believe in a God who removed one of His creatures in so arbitrary a fashion? His sister and I comforted each other and remained lifelong friends.

During this time Bunty was learning to be an actress at RADA, which was a drain on the family purse and turned out to be an emotional drain on her, resulting in a near breakdown. She was sent over to Ireland to stay with an aunt whose husband was trainer to the Aga Khan. There she rode the racehorses on their early morning gallops and eventually made a slow recovery.

The European war at last drew to an end. On VE night we all gathered outside Buckingham Palace and swayed with the joyous crowds, singing and shouting. Later we went dancing at The 400 and in our party was a young Fleet Air Arm pilot with crinkly fair hair. He had just completed his training as a pilot in South Africa and was due to continue the war in the Far East. That night he took me home in his car, an old drop-head yellow Rolls-Royce. Before we said goodbye at the door of the flat he asked for my telephone number.

CHAPTER 16

The young Fleet Air Arm pilot was the younger son of an industrial peer whose ancestors had come to England from Germany in the 1870s. At the time of our meeting his father was seriously ill with heart problems. The elder son, a brilliant scientist, who was to have followed in the family tradition, was killed a few weeks before the end of the war. He was in the Royal Navy and was rejoining his ship when his small seaplane made a bad landing and dived into the water. His body was never recovered. Inconsolable at the death of her elder and favourite son, their mother had been unable to tell her sick husband and was determined that her younger boy should be brought back from South Africa to break the news. Using her influence with Winston Churchill and Lord Cherwell, she arranged that he should be flown back to England on indefinite compassionate leave. She didn't seem to realize or care that he, brought up in his brother's shadow and dazed by his death, was being given an impossible task. He assumed only that his parents would never forgive him the fact that he and not his brother had been allowed to live. But when he entered the sickroom there was no need for words. His father read the tragic truth in his eyes.

He was only twenty at the time, and later told me he bitterly resented leaving the Forces and being made to take over the responsibility of running the family estates, but eventually he became reconciled to the idea. He had done an agricultural course while training to be a pilot and knew a little about farming, but he wasn't ready to step into his brother's shoes. He also had to abandon the thought of taking up the place at Oxford he had been offered when he was at Eton.

Whenever he could escape from the farm he would motor up to London and collect me from the BBC in his open yellow Rolls. He would pour out his heart about all his new responsibilities and hopes for the future. Undaunted by his youth and lack of experience, he believed that by finding new ways of growing certain crops the future course of agriculture could be changed just as much as industry had been changed by the advent of plastics. 'My great-grandfather, my grandfather and dad have all been great scientists and industrialists and politicians. They have all contributed in some way to the welfare of mankind. I want to make my own contribution in my own way.'

Being totally unaware of his family and their history, I listened with fascination. One night, when we were dining at a fashionable restaurant called the Bagatelle, I looked around the room at the overdressed, jewelled women and their suave escorts and said unthinkingly, 'This place is great except for the fact that it's mostly full of rich Jews.' I suppose it was an expression I must have heard frequently and never questioned. A mild form of conventional anti-Semitism had been part of my colonial background.

'You could say I'm Jewish, except that I'm not rich,' he remarked. Blushing and embarrassed by my stupidity, I started a stammering apology. 'Don't worry,' he said, 'I'm used to it.' He took my hand and continued, 'I first became conscious that I was part Jewish at my prep school. My brother told me one day that he was being persecuted. I was mystified, but he explained that his life was being made intolerable by constant bullying and that mine soon would be. He insisted we run away to London to our parents' flat in Grosvenor Square. It was my first awareness of anti-Semitism.' In later years I was to come across my early gaucheness in others and became adept at cutting them short to avoid their embarrassment. Later he gave me his father's book called *Thy Neighbour* about the persecution of the Jews in Europe before the war. It was the most moving account I have read of that vile period and it opened my eyes for ever.

One day he drove me down to the beautiful Queen Anne house in Bedfordshire where the family had moved after leaving a vast Victorian mansion in Hampshire. As we drove over the pretty humpback bridge and down the rhododendron-lined drive I began to feel increasingly apprehensive. He had been quite explicit about his feelings towards me and I knew, instinctively, that today he would ask me to marry him.

The butler had laid out a cold lunch at one end of the long polished dining-room table, and he opened a bottle of champagne. Afterwards we went on a tour of the house. All the furniture was shrouded in dust sheets and gave me a strange ghostly feeling. The magnificent collection of Italian Renaissance pictures, the Bellini Saints, the Guardi and Canaletto scenes of Venice, and the music-room full of Greek marble sculptures, all created the eerie atmosphere of a Cocteau film. We reached the small bedroom he had had since he was a boy. 'I love this room,' he said and led me to the window to see the enormous copper beech rising from the lawn below, its great branches supported by wooden poles. 'That tree knows of all my dreams.' He took me in his arms. 'And now my only dream is that you will live with me forever as my wife.' I drew gently away. I wasn't ready for all this – for love, for marriage. I wanted to live a little, to taste freedom on my own, to explore life by myself, outside my mother's all-enveloping demands. I wasn't in love with him; I loved him like the brother I'd never had. I admired him – his courage and his idealism – more than anyone except my father. Although younger in years, I felt so much older. He seemed unsophisticated and unworldly compared to some of the men in their late twenties I'd been going out with. I procrastinated and tried to tell him some of my thoughts without hurting his feelings. But I knew he would persist.

When we returned to London, I didn't tell my mother what had taken place, but I did tell her that I wanted to go abroad for a while. My friend was leaving the WRNS and taking a job in the Control Commission in Germany. I wanted to join her. My mother was distraught. 'You aren't even old enough to join as an officer – you'll be one of the "other ranks".' She was right, but I was insistent and enrolled as a private in the RDR (Reparations, Deliveries and Restitutions) division of the Control Commission. My new admirer was shattered at first, but accepted that I needed time to make a decision about the future and to be by myself, away from family ties and obligations. He was adamant that he would one day convince me that we should spend our lives together, but he was prepared to be patient. 'I will wait for you, for ever if necessary.' He said he would consider us engaged.

I arrived at Minden, a small German town near Bad Oeynhausen, in my ill-fitting khaki uniform to take up my job as secretary to a Brigadier in charge of the Polish Division of the RDR. My heart sank as we were shown our quarters : a dormitory of army bunks, reminiscent of my school days at Bath. Early the next morning we were woken by a Sergeant-Major shouting, 'Come on, my lovelies, time to rise and shine. The sun'll soon be scorching your eyebrows.' But after the first few days I grew accustomed to the physical discomfort and bad food, and became intrigued by my new adventure.

RDR was set up to restore various properties, factories and goods looted by the Germans from the countries they had over-run. Our particular branch dealt with Poland, and a team of Polish officers was stationed at Minden to liaise and negotiate with us. They were charming men and, when we weren't working, they would take us riding and dancing. Sometimes, if we had a few days off, we would go skiing in the Harz mountains or sailing at Travemünde, north of Hamburg. It was a carefree life for those in the occupying powers but, even at that age, I became very critical of how some members of the Commission misused their power and authority. I was also extremely sorry for the German civilians whose homes we were living in.

Cigarettes and coffee were the black market currency and a few packets of cigarettes could get you a suit made by the best tailor in Minden. I still have a pair of jodhpurs, which cost one pound of coffee, of slightly Germanic cut made by a man who used to make riding breeches for the German cavalry. Some high-ranking officers even abused their positions to furnish their homes in England with carpets and pictures taken from German houses. Many Germans were living in appalling conditions in the rubble of cities, and highly qualified people were performing menial tasks for the Allied Forces.

One day a Polish Count who was one of our negotiators took me out to dinner and asked me if I would like to take part in a little conspiracy. 'You would be doing a great service to Poland,' he said. I wanted to hear more before agreeing, and he explained that towards the end of the war the Germans had stolen the best horses from the Polish stud farms and that they were now in Southern Germany in the American Zone. The Americans were unaware of the true value of the horses which were to be slaughtered to extract a certain serum for medical experiments.

'We want to kidnap the horses,' he said, 'and we happen to know that the order for the execution will be coming through your office in the course of the new few weeks. We would like you to hide the letter until we have returned the horses to Poland.' I didn't hesitate for a moment and entered into the spirit of the adventure.

A few weeks later the Brigadier came into my office. He was a small, gentle man, rather vague, with a neat white moustache. 'Sonia, have you seen a memo about some Polish horses? I'm told, from above, we ought to be taking some sort of action over them – something to do with our American friends.' Looking totally blank, with the letter burning a hole in my in-tray, I said I had no knowledge of any such memo, but told him I would let him know as soon as it arrived. He turned on his heels and went back to his office and to the tapestry he was embroidering for his wife in England. Later that day, one of the Polish officers told me that the operation had been successful and that the horses had been kidnapped from the American zone, taken through Berlin and then by boat across to Poland. Years later the Count, by then living in London, wrote a book about the rebuilding of the Polish stud farms and about a young girl in the Control Commission who had helped to save the horses. The book was printed in a limited edition and privately published.

During this year, my determined suitor was writing long weekly letters and sending from England small luxuries impossible to find in Germany. Particularly welcome were the parcels of books – he sent *Great Expectations*, his favourite Dickens – and food to supplement our monotonous diet of Spam, beetroot, sausages and potatoes. He was living by himself, farming the estates, with only a small black cocker spaniel I'd given him. He was determined we should marry as soon as I returned home after my year of wanderlust. I was in a no-man's land of indecision. I knew in my heart of hearts I would never find anyone I loved and respected more; perhaps these feelings would grow into something deeper.

In the meantime I was madly infatuated with a much older married man. He had been a prisoner-of-war, had escaped and was in the Grenadiers, stationed nearby at Bad Oeynhausen. He gave me very little encouragement but knew how much I cared for him, and we gradually became inseparable. I told him about my life and indecision about the future. 'You should marry him,' he said. 'I will never be able to leave my wife – she is in a mental home.' Apparently she was a very beautiful woman and had already been unstable before their marriage. While he was in the POW camp she became completely insane.

Instead of going back to England for our leave, my girlfriend and I decided we would travel round Europe. We obtained two 'movement orders' and I stamped them with every official stamp I could lay my hands on so that they looked extremely important. Flourished in the faces of bemused German and Italian guards, they took us effortlessly on our train journeys through Germany and Italy. In Venice we stayed in a suite in the Danieli Hotel, which had been requisitioned by the Allies, for a nominal one pound a night. Afterwards we returned via Paris, where reality hit us and we had to conform with the accepted standards of civilized behaviour. But the code of morality practised by the occupying forces in Germany at that time was ambiguous. We had no feelings of guilt or of behaving dishonestly.

In my usual fashion, I was putting off any decision about the future until I returned to England. Once back, all the pressures were on me. In the year I had been abroad the diffident young boy had become a determined and passionate young man, desperately keen to get married as soon as possible. My mother, worn out by her wartime jobs and unhappily reunited with my father, was more anxious than ever that her daughter should escape the limitations of family life and make a 'good match'. To be fair to her, she had become devoted to the intense, pale-faced young man who had used the flat whenever he came up to London rather than stay at his parents' unwelcoming apartment in Grosvenor Square. In the end I succumbed, convincing myself that I would never find a true soulmate in life, so I should marry this boy whom I loved and respected. His need I could fulfil.

In the frenetic preparations leading up to the wedding, I put into the recess of my mind my doubts and reservations. Good clothes were difficult and expensive to find in England at that time, and my aunt in Ireland sent over my wedding dress of white crêpe bordered by tiny pearls. Throughout the night before what is supposed to be the happiest day of one's life, I cried as if I were going to a funeral. In the morning, my mother's remedy was to give me a strong gin which only made matters worse. My friend's cousin had just started a florist business from her home and was meant to go to Covent Garden early in the morning of the wedding to create a spray of gardenias. It arrived with half the flowers turning brown from the fingers of the novice florist. Instead of telling me and letting me walk down the aisle with my ivory-backed prayerbook, my mother handed me the bouquet at the last minute, pretending it did not look like a wreath. As my father led me down the aisle of St Paul's my eyes were glistening like the pearls on my dress. I could not know that soon I would fall helplessly in love with my husband.

In trying to look through the glass clearly and then face to face, in reflecting on the events which seemed important to me as I grew up, I may have been selective and forgetful. But what I have remembered made me the wife I was, the mother I became and the woman I appeared to be after my husband's death. I put away childish things but they have made me the way I am.

PART THREE

Warm are the still and lucky miles,
White shores of longing stretch away,
The light of recognition fills
    The whole great day, and bright
The tiny world of lovers' arms. . . .

Restored! Returned! The lost are borne
On seas of shipwreck home at last:
See! In the fire of praising burns
    The dry dumb past, and we
The life-day long shall part no more.

W. H. Auden,
Songs and Other Musical Pieces, XXXVI

CHAPTER 17

Exactly eleven years and one month after the husband's death she remarried. He was an historian and a novelist, and had recently suffered deeply at the hands of fate and from a hurtful divorce. At the time of their marriage, neither thought they would ever again find peace of mind, let alone happiness. But unbelievably and miraculously they did: gradually at first, discarding their emotional armour bit by bit, and then recklessly as if swept along on a flood of love and desire. They were both taken by surprise by the haphazard inevitability of their meeting and the strength of their feelings. He told her she was the first really honest woman he'd ever met: 'All the others I've known well, except for one, have been inveterate liars.'

But was it true? Until she met him, during the years in between, so much of her life had been a pretence. One of the reasons she had fallen in love with him was that he allowed her the luxury of being completely true to herself. Just as her first husband had released her from her mother's desperate insistence that everything she did in life should be successful, he had shown her that she, too, had the right to fail. Now at last she felt restored. Death and grief were muffled and far away.

He did not want to know of her first marriage. Her dead husband would always be his rival. But she did tell him of the years at the end of her bereavement. They had been full of disasters and pitfalls as well as some minor achievements. Her sister Bunty had died in a tragic accident leaving a distraught husband to bring up three children. The small shy girl who had so bravely jumped the ditch at Dover Castle had become a beautiful and talented woman, only to have her life cut off.

She told him of her own children. Her younger daughter had continued to live at home until the second marriage. A close understanding had developed between them after the initial painful misunderstandings when they had been living out their private hurts, unable to communicate. Perhaps she had been too tolerant. Sometimes parents go on respecting the patterns set by the past in their relationship with their children, and sometimes they veer too much in the opposite direction. In her case, maybe there had been too much freedom and too little parental control. Her daughter later told her that, occasionally, she would have welcomed more guidance. At school she had rebelled when she had been reprimanded, but had accepted it as the natural state of affairs. After leaving school her daughter had gone up to Oxford to take a degree in Art at Ruskin College and had become a dedicated painter.

She told her husband how she had picked up the threads of her past life and had resumed her work for various charities and the contemporary theatre. Sometimes she felt that sitting on the boards of charities was very much like live theatre, while the live theatre was often desperately in need of charity. She had started to entertain again, having an inflated reputation for being a political hostess. But the myth had become fact. People from many spheres of influence gravitated to her house, anticipating and therefore creating the atmosphere of an exciting party where opposing views crossed, romantic liaisons began and occasional events occurred which made headlines in the frivolous press.

The mask she had worn deceived everyone – she was a good actress. She was 'getting over it', her friends said. She had 'picked herself up' and was 'back to normal'. She was in the public eye once more with photographs appearing in the glossy magazines, always smiling. She felt she had to smile into cameras. 'Smile though your heart is breaking' went the song. *Click* went the shutter. And the photographs preserved her, smiling at grief.

Her own mother would have been proud of her. She was 'keeping her end up'. But her mother had died in a bedroom festooned with photographs of her two daughters cut from the magazines. She had sacrificed her life to them, had loved them more than herself and, in her terms, they had 'pulled their weight in life', 'had made the most of themselves'. The death of her mother affected her deeply. In one way a great burden had been lifted – the demands, the dependence, the needs, trying to control the drinking and the smoking, and the responsibility of knowing that she had been the only one capable of bringing any true happiness into her mother's life. But the lifting of the burden left its own void, one less human being needed her love. At least, she consoled herself, in the last declining years her mother had never slipped into melancholia, become bedridden or worried about having to go to an old people's home. She had died without stress.

Her cousin had come to the funeral service in Chelsea Old Church. 'Always have preferred funerals to weddings,' he said. He was still unmarried and had completed two more transatlantic races in the same tiny boat. A man of action and culture, in the mould of his paragon Malraux, he seemed to bring some sanity into an insane world. He had become an integral part of the family. Her elder daughter, now happily married, was working for him as an editor. After taking her degree in Third World Studies and a post-graduate course at London University, she, like so many young women of her generation, had found difficulty in finding a job to fit her qualifications and had resorted to getting secretarial jobs to earn a living. The custom of *primo genitur* operating in

England had left the girls relatively hard-up compared to their brother.

They had all gathered back in the house after the service. 'Let's open the champagne,' her cousin said. 'Your mother would have expected it. She always enjoyed a party.'

Her son in his role as head of the family, poured the champagne into the outstretched glasses. As the corks popped her woman friend said, 'Your mother would have approved – she was always happy when other people were having a good time. She was the most unselfish person I knew.' Her friend had finished her glass in a gulp and held it out to be refilled. She had been fighting a losing battle with alcohol and pills for years. Twice she had been found after taking an overdose of Tuenol and twice had been resuscitated in hospital. Once, when things got totally out of hand, she had been committed to Banstead Mental Home. On a visit there, it was heartbreaking to see her once-beautiful and clever friend sweeping floors in a ward, a vacant expression in her eyes, surrounded by sad moronic creatures. They had sat on a bench in the grounds. It was like a scene from a Beckett play – the non-sequiturs, the broken sentences, the occasional rational phrases. When she was eventually released, her friend was a shell of her former self. The seven sessions of shock treatment had taken their toll and had left her with only half her original personality, but at least she was less disturbed.

But for the grace of God . . . she thought. But apart from the first months of grief she herself had not been tempted along the path of self-destruction. Whenever she had been near to giving in, some fierce pride and vanity had stopped her. Her father would have disapproved: she would be letting down the dead as well as the living. Although she found it difficult to believe in life after death, she had read of countless people who had had the mystical experience of communicating with loved ones in methods of expanding consciousness on to a spiritual plane, but she didn't envy them. She was very much aware of those she had loved being part of the air she breathed. They would enter her dreams at night and keep her company at unexpected moments during the day. But she had a passionate belief in the present, in the philosophy that every moment lived was precious. The first American woman astronaut had said it was important to live today as if you were going to die tomorrow and to work today as if you were going to live for ever. This she believed.

After the funeral service, the drinks flowed and tongues loosened. She listened to her son saying to her cousin, 'I have to give a talk at Cambridge tomorrow on the CND.' They were both supporters of nuclear disarmament, and her son and his girlfriend had recently been photographed in the papers cutting the barbed wire surrounding an American air-field in Norfolk. He was carving out a life for himself as a keen advocate of some of the more controversial left-wing issues of the day and was a leading force in the conservation of the countryside and the attack on the rule of the élite. He prac-tised what he preached. Without faith in any religion or mar-riage, he had a child by his girlfriend, a son who could not inherit the family title that his father believed was an anach-ronism. In the early years she had argued fiercely with her son, believing that his boy should be free to make his own choice, as he had. But realizing how strongly he adhered to his views, she had learnt to avoid controversy and so keep him close to her. Perhaps it was a cowardly solution and a compromise, but she had seen so many families break up because of ideological differences. In moments of crisis and celebration, the family was all-important.

Two years previously she had visited China for ten days. She had been deeply impressed by what she saw. There they understood the importance of the family unit which played its part even within the complex system of the workers' co-operatives. The old were integrated and made to feel a necess-ary part of the community; by being given jobs within their capacity, such as taking care of the young children while their parents worked, they felt needed. There was no such thing as being sent into an old people's home to be an embarrassment to others, or buying their way into expensive enclaves for the aged as often happened in Western countries. For the first time, in China, she had felt that she belonged to an inferior race. The people were all so innately good-mannered and so beautiful that she had felt clumsy and ugly. Perhaps the fact that they had the most ancient culture in the world endowed them with a superior wisdom, grace and self-confidence. Perhaps it had something to do with the yin and the yang of the Chinese character. According to a Sung philosopher, the positive and negative in man are not in conflict, but 'like the whirling water in a confined rocky gorge find a convenient outlet'. Man must be directed to a proper channel.

She certainly felt in total harmony with her second husband. She had heard it said that if you knew too well the person you loved, you killed love, that a certain mystery was essential. But surely the more one looked into the world of knowledge, the more mysteries remained to be solved. And so it was between them. He asked her to tell him about her youth up to the time of her first marriage. She tried to recreate for him her childhood in India and her growing up during the war. She told him, using the simple words that she had used then. If she had used all the words and thoughts she now knew, she could not have told him of how she was then. Someone would have been missing. Herself. When she had finished, he said, 'Now I'm beginning to know you.'

CHAPTER 18

Soon after her second marriage her husband was asked to give a series of lectures in India. His parents also had been in the colonial service and his childhood as unsettled as her own. It was his idea that they should visit her birthplace at Naini Tal in the Himalayas, one of the hill stations at the time of British rule. They both had work to do in America and so they decided to take a delayed honeymoon, a two-month trip round the world finishing in India. It was to be a voyage of remarkable discovery, not only of exotic countries, but of each other. Some places she had visited before; others he knew intimately, but were unknown to her. They might delight in showing each other some of their favourite sights, but best of all would be the formation of a residue of instant memories they would later be able to share.

They drove through Yucatan, along dusty roads lined with thick hedges of yellow daisies. They talked about nothing and everything and, infecting each other's mood, fell into long silences – the silence of accord, not the camouflage of unease or disagreement. He showed her some of the ancient sites he had visited years before when on a sabbatical from Harvard. He had brought his old diaries illustrated in his own vivid primitive style, a little reminiscent of Grandma Moses. They climbed up the Pyramid of the Magician at Uxmal and inside the castle at Chichen Itza to see the Red Jaguar, suffering vertigo and claustrophobia and intense humidity. They listened to the songs of the *mariachis* as they ate *enchiladas* and giant prawns wrapped in bacon and got drunk on Tequila Sunrises and Margaritas. He painted a picture of the Cenote, the sacred pool where human sacrifices were made to the Gods, and he showed her Coba, the centre of the ceremonial roads of Yucatan. They flew to Palenque, the ancient Mayan site on a hill surrounded by rain forests, and they felt overwhelmed by its brooding magnificence and unearthly quality. But she found Tulum the most beautiful of all, its white buildings rising on cliffs overlooking the turquoise sea. They swam beneath the Temple of the Falling God and promised each other they would plunge together into the unknown.

At Los Angeles airport she left her handbag containing their every document in the bus taking them to their hire car. Ashamed and dismayed she thought she had brought their adventure to an abrupt and disastrous halt. He comforted and calmed her. Eventually and unbelievably, the handbag was discovered intact, and they were able to continue. She marvelled at his tolerance and his philosophical approach to misfortune and the strength she felt in his presence. She wondered if he, too, gained strength from her. Perhaps they put on an act for each other which, because they loved, became a natural state of being.

They flew to Australia, crossing the date-line, and felt disorientated as they walked round the Sydney Opera House, which looked like three giant whales stranded on a concrete beach. He bought her an opal ring, and a boomerang for his son.

They spent a week in Bali and swam naked in the sea at night, lying on their backs, their fingers touching, following the path of the low moon and the distant stars – a visit to the universe of which their planet was such a particle. It was a time of inspired selfishness in a place where love could live, and all sense of the hours dissolved. The hotel consisted of a series of chalets and allowed them to cut themselves off from

the world. They ventured out only to see the ballets performed by enigmatic young girls accompanied by twenty-six
piece *gamelan* orchestras, the men sitting cross-legged behind
their instruments. Straight-backed, the girls fluttered their
double-jointed fingers and toes like butterflies. They jerked
their heads and necks from side to side and danced with the
extremities of their bodies, using only their eyes to express
fear and surprise. As they twirled their long skirts between
their legs, they were like animated dolls, their small breasts
bound in gold, children with painted faces and trained
dancers' bodies, beautiful but sexless as they performed their
ancient rituals.

Silently, strolling back along the beach, she and her husband listened to the noises of the night, the lapping of the
waves, the rustling of the tall trees and the distant barking of
dogs. In their hut they found flowers threaded into leaves
lying on their pillows. In the early hours of the morning, they
were woken by the sound of a bird mocking them. They
reached out to touch each other in unspoken comfort against
superstitious fears. Later a boy wearing a green *batik* sarong
and head-dress brought mangoes, hot croissants and strong
coffee to start the day. One time she luxuriated in a massage
of coconut oil and cried out as the giggling Balinese girl
clicked her finger and toe joints. They had a final candle-lit
dinner on their terrace – barbecued fish and duck cooked in
banana leaves – and they drank long cool drinks with waxen
frangipanis floating on the top. They left pieces of food outside their hut that night to appease the Gods, but the following morning at dawn the bird gave his farewell screech to
mock at their happiness.

In Jogjakarta in Java, the atmosphere was oppressive. From
the windows of their hotel they could see the volcanic range
of mountains shrouded in mist, looking like a row of drom-
edaries. Yet the travel that cut their existence into sections
and countries only drew them closer.

Each day they spent together brought new discoveries about their past lives. They never tired of the telling or the hearing. Amazingly they found their paths had crossed on several occasions. Sharing the same tastes in art, music and the theatre, they realized they might have brushed against each other in concert halls, theatres or galleries. The chance meeting that had eventually brought them together had come just in time. He had been thinking, in his state of despair, of leaving England to start a new life in America. He regretted their friends' ineptitude at not bringing them together earlier. This gave an urgency to their love and a heightened awareness to every shared moment. At the beginning of her grief, she had recognized the same heightened awareness. Although they were fascinated by each other's past, it was the present and the future which absorbed them. Their optimism knew no bounds; they would enjoy each day for the adventure it brought, they would plan extraordinary projects for the future. She had heard somebody say that loving meant losing one's liberty and integrity. The reference must have been to a different emotion. It was before she met him that she had felt chained inside her own prison. The prison of suffering she had experienced was only a tiny part of the suffering of mankind and perhaps to tell of it was self-indulgence. But she believed the only real tragedy was to lose hope, to give in to the despair which Catholics believe to be a sin. He told her of some of the times he had been close to despair, not because of death but from living.

When they visited Burma, they stayed first at an old colonial hotel in Rangoon. Its high ceilings, electric fans and atmosphere of decaying gentility reminded her of some of the Indian buildings of her youth. They walked bare-foot round the Shwe Dagon Pagoda and placed flowers in the shrines of their birth signs. The monks welcomed them into their monasteries and young novice monks served them tea in tin mugs, lumps of rough cane sugar, nuts, rice and papayas.

Outside the monastery, an old man was selling rolled horoscopes that looked like ancient scrolls. She wanted to buy one, but the old man needed to know the hour of her birth. She had no idea, but hoped to find it out at the end of the journey in Naini Tal.

In Pagan on the banks of the Irrawaddy, they gazed in amazement at the sight of the thousands of temples and pagodas scattered over the scorched golden earth, the greatest wonder of the East. They visited the holy Mount Popa, the cone of an extinct volcano and the centre of the worship of the Nats, spirits and demons that must be appeased with gifts. On this major pilgrimage, they made their own Act of Merit. He bought a tiny pewter bell with a heart-shaped clapper, which a monk hung in the wind on one of the gold-spiked domes. He said it would tinkle for ever and ever, a memorial to their love.

They left Burma full of admiration for its people, their friendliness, gentleness and generosity; for its beauty and its Buddhist code of morality. *Karma* – not meaning fate as she had always thought – is central to rebirth, each rebirth resulting from Acts of Merit performed in a previous life. She was not yet reborn, but said her prayer of gratitude on her knees in the words of the Lord's Prayer as she had done ever since she could remember.

They eventually reached Delhi, from where they planned their visit to Naini Tal. They paused for two days to rest and clear their minds. The eight-hour drive to Naini brought back to her a host of memories. Nothing seemed to have changed. Dusty streets with Indians frenetically going about their business; the bright saris of the erect women carrying beakers and bundles on their heads; the stalls of fruits, nuts and spices in the villages; the thousands of bicycles; the lorries with the demand 'Horn Please' written on the back, and every driver obeying so noisily. The cows allowed to wander freely through the traffic; bullock carts by the dozen pulling sugar cane to the queue at the factory gates; thin men labouring at their rickshaws. The life of India was on the road in continual frenzied movement. Their driver told them that it was Purima, the Festival of the Full Moon. Tens of thousands of Indians were flocking to the banks of the River Gunja for the ritual washing away of sins.

As they crossed the bridge and watched the masses arriving at the waterside on foot, by bicycle or by bullock cart, she recalled the long car journeys of her youth lasting several days, stopping overnight at guest houses and pulling a horse box behind them. Once on their way back to Nagpur, there had been a frightening incident when they were halted by the police at the crossing of the Yanuna River. The river was in full flood and no one was permitted to cross the flimsy bridge. Exhausted and fretful, they had to wait all night in the car. She had watched sheep floating in the strong current among uprooted trees. Many lives had been lost and people were wailing helplessly on the river banks. Eventually the flood abated in the early hours of the morning, and an old man with a long stick was sent across to try the submerged bridge. Slowly, step by step, putting the stick in front of him into the water, he reached the far bank. They were then allowed to follow.

She was brought back to the present by a screech of brakes as they narrowly missed a lorry brimming over with people like bunches of bananas. After four hours they left the cities and villages behind. The road started winding round the foothills of the Himalayas and then ascended steeply towards Naini Tal. The town itself, built round a lake, reminded her of a Swiss mountain resort out of season, the chalets of corrugated iron looking sad and neglected. They were staying at the Swiss Hotel, which had been recommended by Indian friends. Their driver was sceptical.

'There's a much better hotel,' he said, 'but all the English like to come here.'

She told the charming old proprietor who came out to meet them, 'We've many friends who know you. You're quite famous.'

'Not famous,' he replied. 'Notorious.'

The hotel must have been exactly as it was when her mother had visited Naini – perhaps she had even stayed there.

'I'm afraid we are very full,' the old man said, 'but we have kept a room for you.'

There was a BBC television crew shooting a film about Jim Corbett, the mighty white hunter and local hero whose claim to fame was the single-handed killing of man-eating tigers. There was also a group of British birdwatchers, keen and earnest, armed with binoculars, telescopes and camera equipment. The room they were given was in a tumble-down annexe which made no concessions to warmth or comfort, and an icy wind blew through the broken fan-shaped panes of glass above the door.

Disheartened, they wandered out to walk round the lake. They went through a graveyard and past the church of St John in the Wilderness, long since abandoned. On one of the gravestones they read 'James Gideon Drew killed in the landslip'. One hundred and six years ago, thirty-three inches of rain had led to a catastrophe when the whole mountainside had dropped, burying soldiers and civilians in a living tomb.

'How terrible,' she said. 'It's one thing to have been born here, but I wouldn't want to die here.'

Later that night with the full moon shining through the dusty broken glass, they huddled together for warmth in the freezing room. Her mother had painted such a romantic picture of Naini. She had been heavily pregnant that summer, but there had been flirtatious rides along the bridle paths with young subalterns on leave in the hill station to avoid the monsoon and the heat of the plains. She had told her daughter that she was rather vague about dates and was riding up a steep hill

to the steps of the hospital, where she had started to give
birth.

They found the green-gabled Ramsay Hospital the next
day. It was, indeed, on top of a steep hill overlooking the
lake. She wanted to find the record of her birth and to know
the exact time for horoscopes and fortune-tellers. But the old
Registrar in his seedy blue tunic was doubtful if he could find
anything. In the small office there was a Dickensian chaos
thousands of papers piled higgledy-piggledy in alcoves, or
shelves, in boxes or buried in drawers. Birth and death certifi-
cates were all mixed up together. But, eventually, with a
triumphant flourish, he produced a piece of faded paper
Female Infant – born to Mrs. Graham, wife of Capt
R.H.Graham, R.A.M.C., stationed at British Stations Hospital
Agra.' Sadly, no hour of the day or night was inscribed. She
showed her husband the trophy. Maybe she would never be
able to discover her future in horoscopes, but both felt a
strange sense of fate. He had taken her back to where she had
been born – now they could go on with their journey.